HOW TO
GET ALONG WITH Almost
EVERYBODY

HOW TO GET ALONG WITH *Almost* EVERYBODY

ELTON T. REEVES

amacom

A DIVISION OF AMERICAN MANAGEMENT ASSOCIATIONS

International standard book number: 0-8144-5316-3
Library of Congress catalog card number: 72-92751
First printing

FOREWORD

MANAGERS are a minority group, and they have some special problems. Among these is their heavy responsibility for the success of interpersonal relationships among their subordinates, between their subordinates and the manager himself, between the manager and those in the higher echelons, between the manager and his peers, and with other special groups as they relate to the operation of the manager's sphere of activity. It is the intent of this book to examine these special problems—which have become part and parcel of the managerial load—and to develop a pragmatic approach leading to some viable solutions.

ELTON T. REEVES

TO OUR DEAR FRIENDS,
JOE AND CONNIE ZIEGLER

CONTENTS

WHY THIS BOOK?

MANAGERS are busy people. About 30,000 books will be published in the United States this year. No author has a right to expect any manager to read his book unless there will be something "in it" for him. This book has been written on the premise that any manager will benefit from improving relationships with the people working for him and with him. These goodies will come to him in several forms.

First: The manager's job will be made easier. Every time conflict occurs within an organization, much valuable time is lost in settling the confrontation in one manner or another. An angry employee is quite likely to be less efficient than one who is operating on an even emotional keel. An angry boss may make a bad decision because the flood of extra adrenalin in his bloodstream has impaired his judgment. If good, easy working relationships are maintained, the work flow will be both increased in volume and improved in quality.

Second: The manager will get better and more active cooperation from his people. It is one thing to have things go smoothly; it is a different matter entirely to be able to go to your people, your boss, or your peers and get them to go that extra mile with you that will mean the difference between failure, moderate success, and a smashing victory. Think of it in terms of your own behavior. With whom will you be more cooperative—the man whom you respect and admire, or the one who has consistently been abrasive in his contacts with you? You must know the answer to that one! It is the difference between the negative or neutral approach and the positive one. Ask any salesman about this.

Third: The manager will have more time for creativity and innovation on the job. The job of the manager is changing these days. There was a time when he could "slip into something more comfortable"—like a rut—and go repetitively down the same road, year after year, in the same old manner. Those days are gone forever, in our culture. As a manager today and tomorrow, you are going to be forced to be inventive, creative, and sensitive to the innumerable changes taking place about us every day. You can be a successful manager only when you build some of these changes into your own organization or penetrate new areas in which your enterprise can operate. But this requisite of good management is not just a matter of foresight and "keeping up with the times." The sense of euphoria generated by generally good interpersonal relationships with those about you is in itself a stimulus to more creative efforts. Again, we are speaking of a positive mental attitude.

Fourth: A manager's upward mobility is given impetus by good relationships. All managers who are in any sense of the word realistic know that if all other things are approximately equal, the man or woman who is both *respected* and *liked* will get the nod for a promotion. There is a gross difference, however, between knowing this fact intellectually and putting it to work for you. We are not saying that promotions are popularity contests, but it would be senseless to ignore the weight of this factor in the total evaluation of candidates for advancement to heavier responsibilities.

Fifth: The manager with good interpersonal relationships is in tune with the times. Not too long ago, the stereotype of the American businessman was that of a hard-nosed, insensitive slave driver who literally cared nothing about the people working for him. In fact, to him they had no faces, and existed only as tools to get the product out the door. Today, increased sophistication, better education, and better training on the part of the workforce have made this kind of manager obsolete. The "bull of the woods" boss is as anachronistic today as the mastodon in North America. The manager of the modern scene must have real concern for the expectations and needs of his employees if he is to be a success. This has been proved too many times to be any longer in doubt.

Thus the manager has much to gain by improving his interpersonal relationships. There are basically eleven aspects of these relationships. They will be considered in detail in the chapters of this book, and are listed below.

Interacting up the line. Before a manager can even get his career off the ground, he has to be sure and solid in his relationships with those above him in the hierarchy. Oh, we may have heard of some rare instances when a rebel won his crusade against "the system," but it is their very rarity which makes these noteworthy. So far as you and I are concerned, we had better be pretty good masons in erecting the *roof* of our managerial homes!

Interacting down the line. To give one last gasp of life

to a tired old cliché, any manager is only as good as his people make him. Remember, it takes only a few saboteurs in strategic spots to completely ruin your hopes for success. Your people must be behind you solidly if you expect to achieve your business objectives.

Interacting with your peers. Theoretically, the U.S. Senate is composed of 100 peers plus the Vice President. However, the real truth is quite different. A handful of senators actually control what goes on in that famous organization, through personal influence and the respect of their peers. The same thing is true of businesses and industrial organizations. So long as it does not lead to the sacrifice of personal principle, every manager must be acutely aware of his status among his equals.

Interacting with customers. It would be an insult to both your personal and business sensitivity to harp much on the importance of your customer (client) relationships. In these days of hypertensive competition, your customers have too many sources for your product or service to stay with you unless they can relate to you successfully and consistently.

Interacting with vendors. Your product will never get to your customers unless you have a smooth and uninterrupted flow of raw materials. Vendors are, like you, human beings, and this you must remember at all times. The fact that you are theoretically in the driver's seat is irrelevant. Ask any rodeo bareback rider!

Community interactions. One fact has been slow in emerging, but is now nearly universally recognized by management people. The manager *does* have a social responsibility that cannot be divorced from his job duties. His task here is to see that he doesn't go overboard in this area to the detriment of his regular assignments.

4

Information, outgoing. Before anything else, the manager must be an expert communicator. He must choose, with exquisite perceptivity, the correct kinds and amounts of information that he will pass upward, downward, and laterally. This is the most sensitive facet of his job.

Information, incoming. Today, the manager's job with regard to incoming communications is to winnow the important from the superfluous. This takes a little doing, in these days of EDP and management information systems. We are in danger of being inundated under a flood of information we cannot use effectively.

Interacting with groups. One danger facing the manager is that he will become preoccupied with his *individual* employees at the expense of the group as a whole. Both are important, and balance here is critical.

Building the team. Once he has recognized and adjusted to the needs of the group, today's manager must make a positive effort to get constructive and unified action from it. This is one of the more creative activities he is engaged in on a continuing basis.

Interacting in the matrix organization. The greater sophistication of the workforce calls for greater sophistication on the part of the managerial minority. Our increasingly complex society and its supporting technology make it mandatory that today's manager be aware of new organizational structures as they appear and understand the demands they will make on his ability to relate well to those he works with.

So, let's roll up our sleeves and go to work. OK?

CHAPTER I

INTERACTING UP THE LINE

ANY RATIONAL MANAGER is going to be deeply concerned with maintaining viable relationships with his boss and those farther up the line. Since by definition management is concerned with getting the job done through other people, it can apply to either going up above you or passing the assignments down the line to your people. No constructive effort will be forthcoming when interpersonal relationships become (or continue to be) abrasive.

HE MAY BE WRONG—BUT HE'S THE BOSS

One of the most difficult and dangerous situations that a manager can find himself caught in is to be honestly convinced that The Man is about to make a mistake. What happens to your relationship if you let him go ahead unimpeded? What happens to you if you apparently throw roadblocks in the way of a course he has decided is the correct one? Is there some way you can keep on the right side of him whether or not he makes this wrong decision? To answer these questions, there are several strategies you may consider. Your use of any of them would vary with the specifics of the situation.

First: Make a vigorous presentation of your arguments against his intended course of action—*but do it in private!* No one relishes losing face in front of his peers or subordinates. Hit him hard with logic and data to support your contrary viewpoint, but give him the chance to fall back and regroup without having been publicly exposed as about to perpetrate a boo-boo.

Second: Know when to drop the argument and let him go ahead. After all, he is above you in the hierarchy, and it is assumed that he has in general more experience and know-how than you have accumulated as yet. All sympathies would be with him if your disagreement were to be carried beyond a somewhat hazy but definitive line.

Third: Consider the possibility of delaying actions to keep his decision from being implemented immediately. You, as the subordinate, will in all likelihood be delegated the job of getting the show on the road. It will be a challenge to your creativity and imagination to devise means of delaying the action without being labeled a saboteur. Your hope, naturally, is that in the meantime your boss will discover the error you have spotted and move in to halt the action. If that fortunate event occurs, you will have earned many brownie points as a bonus, whether he admits it or not.

Fourth: With all due caution and smoothness, gather around you some of your peers who agree with you about the inherent wrongness of the proposal, and launch an attack from many fronts. Needless to say, this is going to take some doing, and will require the greatest finesse in handling them as well as him. Most important of all, there must be no overt indications of any concerted action against the boss's decision. You shouldn't even formally verbalize what all of you know you are doing.

Fifth: Make use of your accumulated credit balances with your friends and associates in other departments or disciplines who are involved in the whole process. They have a stake in the matter, too, and again this can be done without the appearance of having openly defied your manager.

Sixth: Most certainly, you should keep in mind that if you question the boss's decision, you must be well prepared to advance alternatives to his proposal. Never be caught in the position of appearing destructively critical. This is equivalent to cutting off your own retreat.

Seventh: Don't leave *your* people hanging. If they are worth having on your crew, they will soon sense the difference in opinion and will be caught in an untenable conflict of loyalties unless you explain your position to them. You are going to have to count on their essential loyalty to you, but you must also give them the freedom to choose logically between your position and that of your superior. This is one of the most critical facets of the quandary in which you find yourself. The important thing is that you shouldn't leave your people in the dark, to draw conclusions that are almost certainly false and may be harmful to everyone concerned.

Eighth: As a last resort, take the rap for your boss, at least publicly. If all else has failed and your man's action is under way, you will in most cases profit in the long run by being the public whipping boy. There are good reasons for this. You will have the complete sympathy and understanding of those who know the real facts. At the same time, as a junior member of the organization, you are not expected to have the expertise of the leader of the group. Mistakes by second-level managers are more easily excused than when made by the head of the group. But your real target is retaining the good will of the person for whom you have undergone all of these trials. If he is at all honest and mature, he will be willing in return to defend you when you make the mistakes inevitable in your future. The expression is quid pro quo.

Let me establish at this point that none of the above courses of action should ever be undertaken if basic matters of your principles are involved. I did not intend to imply this by anything said above; such an implication would be insulting your integrity. Unfortunately, the dilemma of choosing between a morally correct decision and a career-advancing one arises more often than we would like. This book has been written under the assumption that you have the intelligence, experience, and thoughtfulness necessary in the makeup of any manager. Implicit in the situation we have been discussing is the fact that you will have to make a value judgment—or perhaps a series of them. But to this you have become accustomed during your managerial career, so it isn't a new experience.

Your objective, to recapitulate, is to maintain a good working relationship with the person to whom you report. The brunt of this is on your back, but you have become used to that, so what else is new?

The Spectrum—Servility to Arrogance

American business and industry have built into the national scene something we have long been proud of not having: a caste system. Artificial status is inherent in jobs simply because of their position in the hierarchy; this has nothing whatever to do with the real esteem in which people are held when they have earned it by their own actions. You, as a manager, have a fine line to walk in determining what your responses will be to your boss's managerial style. Choosing these responses will require the utmost sensitivity.

As the title of this section indicates, we will be throwing out a gamut of conditions under which you may be operating as a manager. The interpersonal responses you could make under these conditions could range over an entire spectrum of postures.

First: What do you do if your boss is an anachronistic "bull of the woods"? Believe it or not, there are still a significant number of such relics of the nineteenth century. They will usually be found as entrepreneurs, although they are not extinct in other kinds of businesses. Whatever your final decision may be in this context, you must reconcile yourself to living a difficult business life. In most areas of our social milieu we have progressed from the dominant–submissive roles that used to be standard for the worker at whatever level. In essence, such roles boil down to a contest of personalities. Your actions will be determined by your analysis of the individual situations that arise between you and your boss. There will be times when you will confront him directly; there will be others when you will retreat as gracefully as possible. The major objective is to stay in a position where you can still work together.

Second: How do you relate to the "great gray abdicator"? The simple laws of probability will produce a certain number of "managers" in name only. They are the ones who refuse to commit themselves, who will not make the necessary decisions, and who will pass the buck to their subordinates on almost every point of uncertainty. Actually, your situation here is more tenable than with the bull-of-the-woods boss. Because of his own personal weaknesses, your manager here will be less likely to squelch aggressive actions on your part. You can do more engineering in connection with your own managerial activities, and he will not present much effective resistance to your actions.

Third: What is your game plan for acting under a middle-of-the-road manager? Here is a person who has committed himself or herself to a lifetime of business compromise. This does not mean, however, that he will be so willing to compromise in the area of interpersonal relationships. The thing here is to separate completely in your thinking the business from the personal aspects of your relationships. This man is an individual just as you are. You play him straight. Your contacts with him should be as natural as those within your family. Do *not* calculate in advance how you will respond to the cues you receive. Play them by ear. Be natural. Do your thing, with the one proviso that you be honest with this man or woman in every interaction. An atmosphere of mutual respect is very important to this kind of manager.

Fourth: What is your posture with the "human relater"? This is one of the stickier situations you can get into in your work. This person has tunnel vision; he will be thinking more about his "big happy family" than about getting the product out the door. At the same time, he tends to have many personal sensitivities and a grossly enlarged ego, so you can do an inconceivable number of things that will offend him. Because of his own obsession with the "happiness" syndrome, he can be made quite unhappy personally by perfectly innocent acts on your part. This kind of manager will require intense personal study on your part to stay on an even keel.

Fifth: How do you comport yourself with a participative manager? You have just found yourself in heaven on earth. Here is the person who confronts his problems, either "thing" or "human," and settles them on their merits. With this boss you can be perfectly natural. Read him as a person. React as your natural instincts tell you. There will be many times when you will lock horns; that is as right as it is natural. Fight it out, and may the better man win! You don't keep score in this game—your objective is to get the job done, and at the same time to maintain the best of possible relations between you as people.

Sixth: How do you respond to the "new" kind of manager? It is apparent that our proliferating technology, and our transition from the industrial to the superindustrial state, has made necessary the appearance of a new and totally different kind of manager. He is the product of our graduate schools of business administration. This manager is totally involved in quantification of business data and in problem solving by the omnipresent EDP, decision tree, or whatever is the favored method of working with figures. This is the cyberneticist: the one who is seeking the man–machine relationship that is necessary for the continuation of many of our business activities.

This manager has a different approach to interpersonal relationships. He is not really concerned with the human aspects of business, but with a meld of the animate and the inanimate. He has mixed together the man and the machine in a way you and I cannot understand unless we have had the same kind of training and education to which he has been exposed.

This type of boss is the greatest challenge you will have in interpersonal managerial relationships. Your relationships with him will be functional if they contribute to the reaching of the objectives of the enterprise. He couldn't care less about your feelings for him; his concern is for the welfare of the organization. Actually, that must be your concern as well. Perhaps his is the pragmatic approach to the new problems of a changing civilization. Play this manager as you would a brook trout on a reel: Be responsive to every tiny change in the pressure on the line. Take in when he slacks off, tighten the pressure when he dives or takes off downstream.

One last word: Trying these approaches does *not* mean being all things to all people. It means studying every possible kind of manager to whom you will be exposed, and making your own decisions as to how you will interact with each one. This is an important part of your job as a manager in the new industrial scene.

Predicting Your Superior's Reactions

Your own lot as a manager will be made much easier if you are able to predict how your boss will react in a given situation, since you can then plan your own actions more wisely. It would be simplistic to say that all you have to do to reach this worthwhile goal is to "know" your man or woman. That statement is the truth, but it isn't the whole truth. Remember that we are dealing with the most complex mechanism the world has ever known—a human being. So many variables are involved that it would take a lifetime to list them all. The second way of reaching the goal (and a not inconsiderable one) is that you must also *know yourself*. Of the two charges I have just laid upon you, the latter is the more difficult to accomplish. Being human, we look at ourselves with too much bias and ego involvement to be able to make really good judgments about ourselves without years of careful, objective work.

Now that we have apparently put up insuperable obstacles to reaching your goal of being able to predict your boss's reactions, let's examine a perfectly practical way of doing just that.

The first thing to do is to start a log. Keep a record of some sort—in writing—in a secure place known only to yourself. Use the Critical Incident method. When a noteworthy event has happened in your organization, either good or bad, record how your manager reacted to the situation. Be specific. Describe in minute detail the elements of the situation, including both "thing" and "human" factors. *Don't* make the false assumption that "you'll remember." You won't, unless you keep a record.

Second, at roughly regular intervals, go back and study the log as it accumulates, to see what trends and patterns are developing over a period of time. Similarities and differences will begin to stand out in your superior's behavior pattern, and within a reasonable period of time you will begin to get the feel of what you are after. One occurrence does not constitute a habit; perhaps your man will react differently in a similar circumstance later on. It is only when you begin to gather a list of *similar* behaviors that you will have some basis for starting to predict. This data-gathering-and-comparison phase may seem to take an inordinate amount of time and observation on your part, but it is essential to the success of your project.

Third, and here we have a delicate one, you may wish to discuss candidly with your supervisor his reasons for acting as he did at a certain place or time. If you are going to use this gambit, it's better to do it a little while after the fact than to force a discussion at the scene of the action. It may not even be necessary to ask directly. A discussion of an incident may elicit a voluntary contribution of his or her personal reasons for the behavior. It is still true that every person's favorite subject of conversation is himself.

Fourth, begin to make tentative predictions of your manager's behavior in situations that lie ahead of your working group. Record these, too. But make these predictions on the basis of the data you have accumulated so far, rather than by relying on intuition, as most of us do. Then, when the situation has developed, go back to your record immediately and read the box score.

Fifth, make an intensive analysis of your failures. You will not bat like a big-leaguer at first, and you should be mentally prepared for this fact. But in most cases there will be clues as to why you missed the target, and it is important to you to discover these quickly and thereby add richly to your data bank.

Sixth, it is just as necessary that you analyze your successes—perhaps even more so. Were you right by accident, or from a sound judgmental basis? As a manager, you are by nature and training success-oriented, so it is critical to your operation to know why you made those correct predictions.

Seventh, and perhaps most important of all, is to analyze how *you* reacted to your manager's behavior. Were you in sympathy with what he did, or did it offend you? Why? Remember, we are in the midst of getting to understand ourselves as well as him.

At this point, I should make what at first glance might seem to be a digression. The behavioral sciences are "soft." Due to the multiplicity of variables already mentioned, the method of investigation used here is nearly entirely out of phase with the methodology of the "hard" sciences. Rather than using empirical evidence to develop a hypothesis, the behaviorist starts with making a hypothesis and then looks for supporting evidence. It is a sad fact of life that evidence turned up which does not support the basic theory may be suppressed or entirely ignored. This is the inherent danger in trying to reduce human behavior to scientific theories. Because of our human fallibility, we are nearly incapable of being completely objective when we are ourselves involved in the action. It is for this reason that I insisted from the beginning that you gather all possible data *before* trying to make any predictions about what your boss would do in any given scene. Work with facts, not with wishful thinking.

Let's close the circle. It will be of inestimable value to you to be able to predict what your manager will do in any given set of circumstances. You can thereby order your own business life much more neatly and easily. Your efficiency quotient will be notably improved; you will have more time for the creative parts of your fascinating job.

There is a completely logical corollary to what we have been saying here. You should give every aid and comfort to the efforts of your subordinates to employ the same process with you. They need to predict your behavior just as much as you need to know what *your* boss will do. Explain the process to them; get them involved in the same search for understanding that you have embarked on.

As a member of management, you are also a member of a minority group. It is a quite select and favored group, but it is a minority—perhaps 10 percent of the total workforce. Your membership in it implies some heavy responsibilities as well as some rather spectacular benefits. These revolve principally around your interpersonal relationships. The man on the lathe has only one person to whom he is responsible—his boss. As a manager, you have multifaceted interpersonal responsibilities radiating in all directions from you.

The Dichotomy of Membership in a Hierarchy

The majority of American businesses and industries are still organized in the pyramid structure of successive layers to which we have been accustomed. (This may change, as will be discussed later, but up to now, this is it.) As a member of management in a hierarchy, you have a split personality, whether you recognize that fact or not.

The dichotomy arises because it is necessary to conform to major company policies and directives. Unless you do this, and with pretty consistent appearance of good grace, you will incur the displeasure of those above you. There are good reasons for this, both personal and arising from the group. Top management promulgates that policy which it feels will be most functional in keeping the group on line toward its objectives; anyone who fails to follow this path will have to be punished for deviating.

Your boss has a vested interest in your behavior: His success will be measured in large part by whether *you* succeed or fail, since he is responsible for your career and your behavior. If he observes more than a very few failures on your part to follow the habits and customs (i.e., policies) of your organization, he will feel threatened and your relationships with him will be endangered.

Deviance on your part from the established norms will

also put your subordinates in danger. They will be confused and frightened. Should they follow you, their immediate leader, or should they put themselves in the trying circumstance of having to be seemingly disloyal to you in order to conform?

But the real problem is that this necessity to follow the rules may be in direct conflict with your own self-expression. You may not *want* to do certain things expected or demanded of you, and this may lead to inner turmoil that is upsetting to your mental and emotional stability. Most people have a basic need to be true to whatever mental image they have developed of themselves. We don't like to be forced to act differently from our self-image; to do so makes us feel uncomfortable or resentful. This in turn intensifies our need to disobey the rules that have angered us in the first place, and we have completed a vicious circle.

There are some things we can do about this situation when we find ourselves apparently entrapped. Of primary importance is a period of self-examination to determine whether we actually are violating deeply held principles or whether our rebellion is perhaps a bit juvenile and should be suppressed. Maybe we're just acting like Johnny, petulantly rebelling against his parents' insistence that he dress up before he goes to Sunday school.

If we do make this introspective examination and still come up with a fundamental disagreement with the rules involved, the next step should be an immediate exploration of the matter with your manager. You should at least make clear to him what your difficulty is, and why it is so hard for you to conform. You are a responsible and respected member of your company's management. If it is discovered that several other managers share your feelings about this particular thing, it is not at all impossible that there might be a reevaluation of this bit of policy leading to its eventual removal from the manual. You may not win 'em all, but you won't lose 'em all, either.

Should your immediate supervisor, however, remain adamant, there is nothing wrong with carrying the discussion a step or two further up the line—just so long as you inform your boss of your intention to do so. If they see some point in your objections, most reasonable men will respect you the more for having the courage to carry on the fight.

It is important to note that in this situation there is a point at which your intuition should warn you to drop the matter. The difference between "determination" and "stubbornness" can be tiny indeed. If you step over this line, you may have irrevocably destroyed a working relationship with your manager, and perhaps some others higher up. This is the one result you naturally want to avoid at all costs.

The difference between complete self-expression on the job, which is rarely possible to achieve, and total subjugation of self to the needs of the organization, is a burning question among today's managers, especially the younger ones just now coming into positions of influence.

Some authorities believe that within a few years (if it is not already here), we will see managers displaying a vastly different attitude toward this subject. They will be much more demanding about freedom of action. They will insist on shorter workweeks, as exemplified by the four-day week, so that they will have more time to spend with their families and in personal recreation. Those who advocate this change argue that managers' work efficiency will actually be improved because they will be achieving better personal balance, and that their personal growth and development will be enhanced by a widening of what has been tunnel vision.

Each member of management is going to have to make up his own mind on this matter. But arriving at an opinion on this will not enable any given person to become completely autonomous in his personal actions. The organization as represented by the hierarchy will not have abdicated its position of power, and eventually you may have to decide for yourself between modifying your own behavior and perhaps even severing your relationship with the enterprise. These career decisions are never faced lightly; be sure that you have weighed carefully all possible outcomes before you do this.

These complexities of interpersonal relationships up and down the hierarchy are a product of our social structure and the culture itself, which has become incredibly complex within the memory of most of us alive today. How each of us reacts to this sometimes chaotic scene is a measure of our ability to remain functional as a manager.

FRIENDSHIPS VERSUS BUSINESS RELATIONSHIPS

There are few more troublesome or debated problems in management than the problem of where friendship ends and impersonal business relationships start among managers in the same enterprise. A related question is whether it is possible to mix them, at least to some extent.

There are several considerations here. First, it is entirely possible that the person to whom you are now reporting may have been a member of your peer group until his promotion, and that you were close personal friends during that time. How will his elevation affect your personal relationship? Well, he *is* now your boss, and common sense would dictate that he should be the one to "set the pace" as far as your future socializing is concerned. For the first few weeks or months after the change in the hierarchy, you should be neither too overtly friendly nor too reserved, but assume rather a neutral stance. His actions will give you the necessary cues to set the pattern for the future.

Be prepared for a human disappointment, and consider yourself lucky if it doesn't happen. There are many managers who feel it is impossible to maintain proper "control" over their group if they socialize with them informally. If your new boss is of that sort, give him the courtesy of respecting his thinking, even if it does hurt a bit to see the deterioration of an old close friendship. That's the way things go sometimes.

Second, it would be foolish to maintain a stiff-necked or standoffish attitude if your boss, or his boss, makes overtures of real personal friendship toward you. This must be a signal that they see no contradiction between fraternization and the maintenance of a correct business relationship. Some organizations evince wide differences over their whole structure in this respect. Some actively foster closeness among the managerial groups; others virtually insist on impersonality and the keeping of a "proper distance" socially among their management people. Surely by this time you are capable of reading what sort of general policy your company follows in this regard.

Third, be prepared to maintain a dual personality concerning this matter of social interactions. Some managers think it the best course to remain coldly impersonal on the job, then after hours to cast from them all matters pertaining to business and assume an entirely different personality. If they take this approach, it is probable that they will insist on a "no business after hours" policy when you are together socially. If you can handle this kind of mental readjustment, it can be a pragmatic arrangement. Actually, it is quite a natural and normal thing. Almost all of us have different personalities at home with our family than we have at work, and this is right and proper. They are two different lives.

Fourth, remember that for the sake of organizational unity and good relations with your superior, it is probably better to maintain the same attitude toward your subordinates as has been established by your manager. Whenever possible, continuity of climate should be unbroken up and down the line. At the same time, it would be worthwhile to have open discussion about this with your people, so that any appearance of manipulation or patronization would be avoided.

This entire matter revolves around a central goal—maintaining proper morale and discipline within the working group. The fact that we would *like* to socialize more—since we do spend the majority of our waking hours on the job—is irrelevant to the question. We must weigh our own wishes about interpersonal relationships against the exigencies and demands of the job.

To go back for a moment, I said before that the pressures of our modern culture seem to be pushing us toward a shorter (and perhaps more intensive) workweek. If we can retain the proper mental set toward this, it will result in more fully integrated personalities for everyone. More self-actualization will be possible, we will lead richer and fuller lives, and we will be the better for having grown and developed in more than one segment of our lives.

Once again, it is necessary to indulge in a little introspection. It is up to each manager to determine for himself just how well he can adjust to a mixture of apparently disparate elements in his interpersonal relationships. Is he going to have one set of interactions on the job, and another, with a completely different group of people, off the job? Can he develop a judicious mixture between these two elements? Only you can answer these questions as they apply to you.

To recapitulate, this first chapter has taken a look at some aspects of "human relations" *up* the hierarchical line. As a manager, you must be constantly aware of the shades and nuances of these interactions, both positive and negative, and make quick, sure evaluations of how they will affect your ultimate goals, both personal and those of the organization. The single most important yardstick to keep constantly beside you is your own personal integrity. With the mobility that good managerial talent has these days, and will continue to have in the foreseeable future, it is never necessary to sacrifice personal principles in order to maintain equilibrium in a given organization. You can always go elsewhere.

However, there is obviously another side to this coin. It may be a real challenge to you to buck the system in a given enterprise and impose your will, even on the majority. One of the best indications of your intrinsic value to your employers is your ability to remain inflexible in what you consider to be right and proper in the matter of friendship versus business in your associations with those above you. Some company presidents have gotten where they are by the simple process of being their own man, letting company policy fit itself to *their* concept of what the integrated person should be and how people in the company should behave. There is still a residue of respect left in the heart and mind of every American for good old Yankee independence, especially in matters that are primarily personal. If your track record on the business side is clean, executive placement services will be glad to take you on if the ultimate decision goes against your revolt.

That will probably not be necessary. Part of the "management decision" you made when you first became a supervisor was to recognize the necessity of striking a proper balance between your personal life and that part of your life which belongs to the organization.

CHAPTER II

INTERACTING DOWN THE LINE

As THE TITLE INDICATES, this chapter will examine a reversal of the roles that the manager played in the preceding one. Although your managerial style may not vary, your situation does, and this will modulate your behavior with your people on the job.

Now You Are the Boss

Remember that in general your people will have much the same attitudes toward you that you have toward your superior. They will be asking the same questions about you that are in your mind concerning the person to whom you report.

First, since you initiate much of the action within your group, by means of taking the lead in establishing goals and objectives and supervising the concomitant work assignments thereafter, you will have to be especially alert about what happens to interpersonal relationships during these activities. The managerial function of directing involves interfaces between human beings that can give rise to abrasive results unless special care is taken to avoid them.

Second, you must be prepared for surprises in how your

people react to the things you do as a manager. In a given situation, you may assume that your people's behavior will be perfectly predictable only to find that they go in an entirely different direction as the action commences. This will be traumatic for you unless you are mentally prepared for this sort of possibility. The keys to resolving this problem are fast reaction time and personal adaptability.

Third, it is your responsibility to set the tone in interpersonal relationships within your group. The cues you give your people—oral, written, and nonverbal—must be designed to be read with as little misinterpretation as possible. Never assume that your actions and the thinking behind them are so clear that they cannot be misunderstood. The leader must have a much greater ability to emphathize than the follower.

Fourth, as the boss, you are constrained to referee, or arbitrate, the interpersonal differences that arise among the members of your group. This delicate duty will be demanding of your time and will require your best thinking, if your people are to be formed into a functional team that will get the job done every time on time.

New attitudes and mental sets are appearing in the people who have just recently entered the workforce. Their questioning of authority itself is much more profound and deeply rooted than in previous generations of working people. The manager can no longer assume that positional authority alone will make him functional. He will stand or fall by the amount of *inner* authority he can generate and maintain with his people. You, as the boss, will have to establish this on a one-to-one basis with your people before they will become a working group. One significant factor is the amount of your patience. You will need to go much more than halfway if you wish to generate ongoing, lasting rapport.

Under these new conditions, when you function as an arbitrator of your people's differences your role will contain much less adjudication than it will persuasion and reasoning. This is not to say that you will never be forced to make a decision and say: "This is the way it's going to be!" But that situation will arise much less frequently than it used to in American business.

Fifth, your position as leader assumes that you will be the model for overall interpersonal relationships in the group, both laterally among the members and vertically between you and them. Once they have accepted your leadership, they will expect you to behave like a leader. Your influence over the group norms will be much greater than that of any individual, or group of individuals, on your team. This, of course, will work to your advantage, and your selection of proper normative behavior will be one of the principal indications of your overall success as a manager.

Lest there be a misunderstanding, I should pause at this point to emphasize that your objective is not necessarily an atmosphere of "sweetness and light." After all, your working group is not a fraternal organization, and your main objective will not be solely to satisfy the social needs of those working with you. If strong and lasting friendships arise among your group, this is an extra little goodie for which you should be thankful, but the goal is the absence of friction rather than the presence of euphoria without end. If considerations of friendship become the paramount issue, productivity can only become a casualty.

Sixth, you should never lose sight of the fact that you and your people are human beings, and that in the natural course of things events will arise which demand disciplinary action. Your handling of these events will make or break the overall tone of interpersonal relationships within your group. Let us assume that your previous experience has made you adept at maintaining objectivity throughout such incidents. This is only half the story. After the knuckle-rapping has occurred, there remains the matter of mending the tear in the interpersonal structure, not only between you and the person who has been disciplined but among the other members of your crew as well. Some degree of polarization is inevitable among the membership as they choose up sides in their opinions on the fairness of the discipline levied. It will take days and weeks of work on your part to heal these breaches in your working-group structure.

To recapitulate, as a manager you have special duties and heavy responsibilities in setting the tone for relationships within your group. These are ongoing; you cannot do the job once and relax. In today's culture change is so rapid that what was viable yesterday can easily become dysfunctional tomorrow. Your mind must be on a continuing red alert for variables that can adversely affect the tone of your group. Your ingenuity will be constantly taxed to avoid or defuse the booby traps that will inevitably arise along the route to your group objectives. This is one of the duties for which you have been tabbed as a manager, and for which you receive your paycheck.

How Well Do You Know Your People?

There is simply no way a manager can have any control over interpersonal relationships within his group unless he knows his people well—as individuals. Nor can he hope to come close to influencing the actions of his subordinates unless he is aware of what motivates each of them. The immediately apparent corollary to this is that each employee must be approached as an individual; it is "down the tube" with the old shibboleth that "we have to treat all our employees the same." Policies should be the same, of course, but the manager should be sensitive to special conditions in applying them. Individual differences are so great as to make uniformity of approach impossible—not to mention undesirable.

The question of how much time to allot to getting the necessary data is not inconsiderable, and it has to be solved by every thinking manager. The manager must also settle on a strategy. He certainly can't depend on a haphazard approach, trusting to luck that his fortuitous contacts which result in personal conversations will do the trick. They will not. The manager will have to plan and contrive them on an orderly basis. Of course, part of this planning will involve seeing to it that every one of his employees gets "equal time" in the matrix of his contacts.

There is one thing this project has going for it: All of us are human enough to enjoy talking about ourselves. If the boss evinces interest in us, we are not likely to be curious about his reasons and will probably be only too willing to dish out the data. If you think over these conversations later, it will probably occur to you eventually that the boss keeps probing about what makes you tick—about your motivation. The scene has been set for this sort of thing by the rapid rise of regularly scheduled performance reviews and the commonness of career planning between the employee and his manager. A few rounds of these conferences can give the boss enough information—and some to spare—to be able to predict his people's reactions to a given set of circumstances.

There is, most certainly, one grave caution that any man-

ager engaged in getting to know his people better should observe. Individuals have greatly different thresholds at which
they feel their privacy is being invaded. The manager must
realize that the employee will turn off completely if this point
is passed; he must cultivate a fine intuitive sense and read
well the cues given to him as he approaches the danger point.
There is no possible way to repair the break in a relationship
that occurs when an employee thinks his manager is prying.

As individual backgrounds begin to emerge and take
shape, there will be a real enrichment of your ability to make
work assignments that will be more functional for your group.
This is aside from, of course, the matter of your employees'
technical knowledge, about which you already are well enough
informed. I am speaking of those other interests and skills
that you were unaware each of your people had. This enlarge-
ment of possibilities for re-formation of the group's work will
make for a better organization in all senses of the word. The
added versatility alone may give you flexibility in meeting
many new situations.

If there is the slightest doubt about the advisability of
probing into a certain area, it should not be done. Better to
proceed a little more slowly; the desired information may be
forthcoming voluntarily at a later date. The important thing
is to establish a climate in which the employee will be accustomed to speaking of his own objectives, hopes, and desires
freely and easily. To reiterate: He must be sure that you
are sincerely interested in him as a unique individual, and
he will then be predisposed to give you what you need.

Actually, you will probably discover that the huge time
involvement you feared in doing this job will not materialize.
As much as anything, the task is accomplished by the mental

set you acquire in the pursuit of getting to know your people. When you are thinking along these lines, your daily contacts will become much more meaningful, and your own interpretation of work incidents will add bits to the mosaic that will complete the picture.

It would be eminently unfair of you to refuse to make this sharing of personal information a reciprocal thing. If you are, in a sense, demanding that your employee bare his deeper feelings and thinking to you, you owe him the same privilege. The men and women working for you are at least as curious about you as you are about them. (In fact, you can assume that they are more so, for you are the most important person in their working life.) People are beginning to understand and apply this fact, and it will have—is having—a profound effect on the structure of American business organizations. The relationship that used to be inherent between "boss" and "subordinate" is undergoing gross modification. The more we understand each other, the more difficult it becomes for one person to assume superiority over another, for each of us has so many facets that it is impossible for any one person to be significantly superior to any other person in every aspect. We have our tradeoffs of strengths and weaknesses.

Already this is showing in some enterprises (Texas Instruments is a good example) in a deliberate effort on the part of the executive echelon to blur the differences—especially in status—among the tiers of the hierarchy. We are coming to understand the eternal verity that for any organization success lies in a team effort, and that the best team will be built and led by leaders who understand the players best. Ideally, as we become more sophisticated and as management approaches more nearly the goal of a real profession, the relationship among employees will become that of "colleague." This is not to say that the leader will abdicate in any sense; he will still be responsible and accountable. But his people will be freed from any constraint of subservience, and working relationships will become much freer and more functional.

How Do You Handle Jealousy?

If you have normally ambitious subordinates, there will be jealousies among them. Some will be jealous of each other; some will be jealous of you; some will be jealous of both. The manner in which you handle these situations will be critical to the overall success of your group relationships.

There are some techniques for handling jealousy that every manager should know. First, and extremely important, is to be sure that the ill feelings did not arise from preferential treatment (real or imagined) on your part. You can't afford to have even the appearance of according special consideration to one of your employees. This problem arises most often from your method of work assignment. It is the most natural thing in the world to give a job to the person whom you believe can handle it the best. But this will mean that your most talented personnel will wind up with the challenging jobs—the plums that everyone would like a crack at. It might be more functional for the efficiency of your group if you were always to follow this pattern, but it is dynamite for interpersonal relationships, and fatal to the general growth and development of the less gifted members of your group. Every person needs an occasional "stretch" assignment to test his untapped potential and see how far he or she can really go.

Second, if jealousies are overtly expressed, you should confront them. Here is the best chance you will ever get to improve your own skill in counseling, while at the same time making a frontal attack on a serious personnel problem. You should usually approach each of these sessions differently, depending on your knowledge of yourself and the employee. With some you can be brutally direct, while with others you will skirt the problem delicately by indirection until you can draw out their feelings. Others will fall somewhere between these two extremes. What makes or breaks these sessions is your care to ensure plenty of time and complete privacy in your meetings. Actually, they are much better done away from the work area—in a "neutral corner."

Third, of course, there must be frequent and careful followups after the counseling session. Above all, the people concerned must not be allowed to build up a defensive wall between them that will make it impossible to continue a normal working relationship. This is too destructive of cooperation. As their manager, you have control over their working contacts to a large degree; you can see to it that they are forced to associate on the job, and you can then monitor their interactions on a continuing basis. If you see abrasiveness again emerging, you may decide to hold a meeting with both of them simultaneously. Such mini–group therapy sessions are of the utmost delicacy and will require every ounce of expertise you possess to keep them on a positive plane.

Fourth, and much more difficult to handle, will be those situations where the jealousy is not openly shown but you suspect that it exists. Here you must "build your book" with the utmost care, so that when you are ready to confront those affected you can overwhelm them with documentation of your judgment. If, as often happens, the person does not consciously feel he is jealous, the revelation can have a shattering effect on his composure. As he does openly examine his feelings, his ego will suffer severely for a time, and this is when you should offer extra supportiveness while he is rebuilding his personal defenses. It is important that he not be left feeling degraded in your eyes, or less a man or woman for possessing what are very natural human feelings. Periods of recuperation from these personal traumas will vary widely in length.

Fifth, and hardest of all, will be your methodology for handling jealousies among your people directed at yourself. There are many reasons why these occur. Simplest of all is human resentment at what they feel to be your "superior" position in the hierarchy, and the greater salary and power they know you have. Some vestige of this resentment will always be present in every normal human being; it is your job as a manager to minimize its effect on your working relationships.

A second type of jealousy from below is that exhibited by an employee firmly convinced that he or she is at least as qualified as you are to hold your job. They may be, in fact. The most disarming method of treating this problem is to demonstrate by words and action that you are genuinely interested in their growth and development, and are actively working for their advancement in the hierarchy. If your own upward mobility is temporarily stymied, this kind of work may actually result in your losing some good people from your group, but at least they will go with friendly feelings toward you, and with their personal loyalty to you enhanced many times. The number of friends you have among your peers and colleagues can never be too great.

To summarize, jealousy is one of the most common emotions and has always been present in men; there is no reason to expect it to disappear from our midst in the foreseeable future. As a manager you will have to learn to live with it and to be prepared to treat it, at least symptomatically, whenever it appears.

Concurrently, you could do much worse than to examine your own jealousies, and to estimate how vigorous they really are. Jealousy is stultifying; it can rob us of both intellectual and physical vigor. When our adrenal glands are continuously being overworked, we have no reserves left for the true emergency when it appears. Good judgment can be fatally impaired under the effects of this emotion, since it practically precludes any possibility of objectivity toward its object. The disease—which it is—is always dangerous, and can be fatal to a business career if allowed to go unchecked and untreated. In the final analysis, only you can be the judge of how many people you are jealous of; a simple tabulation of their number and identities may be shocking enough to force emergency mental therapy.

Well, no one ever told you that the practice of management was an easy vocation.

How Not to Become a "Heavy"

American management personnel have for about a generation and a half been increasingly conditioned to consider their people as individuals with thoughts and feelings, rather than as cogs in a machine or adjuncts to production equipment. The manager has become sensitive to any accusation that he is less than aware of his role as a relater with people.

Two dangers are inherent in this situation. The first is that he becomes a "human relater" at all costs, and abdicates his position as a leader of his group members. People loom so high on his personal priority list that he may forget he still has a primary duty to the profitability of the enterprise. He overreacts to cues from his subordinates that they are less than happy with a less than perfect business surrounding. He forgets that he has been hired, and is continuing in his position, just because this situation will never exist.

The second—and polarized—possibility is that he changes into a stuffed shirt. In trying to maintain a rigid balance between "people" problems and "thing" problems he fails in both areas, and is seen by all around him as a schoolmarm rather than as an effective leader and manager.

Relax. There is a solution. Cultivate, and maintain, a sense of humor. Make sure you direct it toward yourself even more often than you direct it toward those with whom you associate. No man or woman can become stuffy who can recognize those times and situations where they look funny to others. If we are the first to laugh at ourselves, others will laugh with us rather than at us, and this is very important to our status and esteem among our associates. Laugh even when it might hurt a little.

Nowhere is this more important than in relations with labor unions. The coming years will see a burgeoning of union membership in the office ranks—and also the professional ranks—of employees. As we are transformed ever more swiftly into the superindustrial state and as manufacturing ceases to be the center of American business and industry, it will be vital that managers become expert in labor negotiations to the fullest extent of their capabilities. However, labor relations will undergo changes so great that they will hardly be recognizable as such to the practitioner of today. Instead of trying to attribute all grievances and discontent to materialistic bases, we will have to take into account an employee's malaise because he is not satisfying some of his social, ego, or self-actualization needs. This change is surfacing even now. But if an employee is hurting in these areas today, the only recourse he has is to file a grievance that will carry some sort of monetary or materialistic award if he wins the battle. The trouble is, these awards will not really satisfy him, and he will continue to suffer after he or she has "won" the case.

So we must be prepared to vary our approach to confrontations between management and labor. One very useful approach is to be alert to every single facet of the situation that presents some humorous aspects to the candid observer. Proper injection of gentle and insightful humor into the discussion at exactly the right moment will provide the fulcrum for the successful resolution of countless problems.

At the same time, every manager must resist with everything in him the possibility of acquiring the reputation of a "heavy" among his peers or those above him in the hierarchy. Of course he will not want to be known as a clown, but of the two choices, it would be less dangerous to a managerial career to have that reputation than to be known as a person totally devoid of a sense of humor. Most people distrust the man or woman who can't laugh.

There is a significant relationship between this human trait and our general physical health. Humor is the perfect safety valve for releasing the pressures within us engendered by our day-to-day struggles on the job. For more than half a century, one of the most popular features of *Reader's Digest* has been "Laughter—The Best Medicine." It is perhaps significant that right now the most popular program on television is a situation comedy about a bumbling bigot who yet retains the saving grace of being able to stand back and laugh at himself once in a while.

Laughter not only has therapeutic effects on the physical health of the manager; it also is beneficial to his mental health. Any human being who consistently takes himself too seriously is flirting with a neurosis or even a psychosis.

Students of humor tell us that its essence lies in the juxtaposition of two antithetical elements, each of which is in itself perfectly normal. The laws of probability will make this happen several times a day in a normal person's life. Development of a sense of humor is accomplished by being constantly alert to these situations and then communicating them with our fellow beings. A chuckle or a belly laugh enjoyed and shared by two people is the quickest catalyst to a good and lasting relationship.

Although this warning is probably not necessary, I should point out the dangers of *over*cultivating this attitude. We do not want to be known as humorless, but neither do we want to be perceived as a person who can never be serious. One hallmark of general managerial sense is the ability to sense intuitively the fine line separating these two extreme positions, and then to walk that tortuous path as a way of business life.

Above all, do *not* become the kind of manager who is incensed when his employees fail to erupt into uproarious laughter at the faintest hint of humor on his part. Things are funny in varying degrees to different individuals, and we must remember that what will fracture one person will elicit nothing more than a faint smile from another. This is as it should be. If we were all alike, what a hopelessly dull existence we would all lead in both our business and our private lives!

TRUST AND CONFIDENCE

Modern business and management jargon has associated these two words like "ham and eggs" or "Smith and Wesson." We breathe platitudes and clichés by the ton about the utter necessity of establishing trust and confidence between the employee and the manager, but only too seldom do we stop to examine with a truly critical eye the methods for achieving this special kind of rapport.

Forty years ago, 98 percent of the management in this country was pure Theory X. That meant that the manager approached his people with the assumption that they were untrustworthy because they hated to work. He found himself right in a sad majority of cases, because we all have a tendency to respond to others in a manner similar to the way they approach *us*. This meant there could be no real trust between the two adversaries—which they were, in the most real sense of the word. In the past generation and a half, a significant percentage, but even yet hardly half, of our managerial population has gone Theory Y. Under the assumptions of Theory Y, the supervisor believes that his people are normally decent individuals, are ready to follow good leadership, and not only desire to work but have an inborn *need* to work to express their individuality to the fullest. In other words, the Theory Y manager is prepared to exhibit trust and confidence in his people, at least until they prove him wrong in a specific case. Once again, he finds that he is right—most of the time.

As in most other work situations, the manager has a greater responsibility in this than does his employee. It is up to him or her to make overtures that indicate he has a deep-seated belief in the probity of his organization's members. He sets the climate. He will never be trusted until he is ready to trust in turn.

We should make a clear distinction here between trust and liking. It is entirely possible for a person to work for someone whom he despises personally but whom he trusts and respects. Conversely, many are the people we have met whom we liked well enough but could never think of trusting for a moment. This is one of the aspects of human nature that makes group living exciting.

There are a couple of cases that should be considered separately. The first is the possibility of the manager of good will getting a new employee who has been badly burned several times by what he considers to be betrayal by former bosses. These people will take special handling—special therapy—and will be slow in changing their attitudes toward supervision in general. With these people, you will have to *prove* yourself worthy of their trust.

The second situation has to do with two segments of the new workforce: disadvantaged employees and modern youth. For so many generations that it has become virtually a self-perpetuating cycle, the disadvantaged employee, now coming into our workforce in ever increasing numbers, has been conditioned to hate, distrust, and fear any authority symbol. And, of course, you as a manager are just such an authority figure. It will probably take many, many months of careful handling of this person before he will begin to believe you and trust you. The National Alliance of Businessmen, in their JOBS program, has allowed for this problem by interposing a counselor between the disadvantaged employee and his supervisor. The major function of this counselor is to engineer and supervise the transfer of trust from himself to the supervisor. The key words here are patience and understanding. A solid book of successful incidents must be written between the employee and his boss before the employee's cultural imprinting begins to fade and he accepts you as a human being.

As for the other segment, Margaret Mead says of our modern youth that this is the first generation in this or any other civilization of which we have any record that has "nothing to learn from its elders." The shock value of such a concept is good for our thinking, although reflection and continued examination will show that it, like any other generalization, is dangerous if carried too far. True, today's younger generation is the best educated, best trained, and most sophisticated of any which has entered the workforce, but there are some fundamentals that *every* generation must learn from its elders. Honesty. Probity. Acceptance of responsibility. Fundamental value sets. Ethics and morality. The fact that our young people have learned so much in so short a time does not necessarily mean that they have learned the right, or basic, things, and we cannot abdicate our responsibility to see that they do get these basics ingrained into their consciousness.

As a manager, it is entirely possible that you will get in your workforce one or more youths who have never in their entire short lifetimes had to face up to a responsibility, or who, for various reasons, have found it impossible to trust or respect the older people with whom they have associated. Here you will have to take on an extra load of managerial responsibility. To some degree, these young men and women are emotional cripples, and must be retrained and taught the basic fundamentals of interpersonal relationships for successful living. Happy landings, captain!

To recapitulate, this chapter has focused on the basics of relating to those at lower levels than yours in the business hierarchy. Underlying the whole situation is your heavier responsibility as the leader; it is expected that you will understand and accept this situation, and will be ready and willing to go more than halfway in working out viable relationships. But there definitely are rewards in this for you. The extra effort will be more than repaid as you develop a smooth, functional, cohesive work group, and your security and effectiveness will be increased exponentially as these relationships solidify and ripen under your leadership. In addition, the psychic income gained from your success in this area will make all the effort much more than worthwhile.

CHAPTER III

INTERACTING WITH PEERS

OUR RELATIONSHIPS with our equals in the hierarchy are quite different from our relationships with those above us and below us in the line. In some ways they are easier to maintain; in others, much more difficult. These differences are due to many factors, some of which will be examined in this chapter.

FRIENDS OR ENEMIES?

If you have been promoted into management within your own line, there are a number of permutations and combinations possible in your relationships with other managers. It is not at all improbable that one or more of your new peers were in former times your boss or bosses. This has two possible implications. If your relationship with your former supervisor was a good one, this person will be predisposed to be friendly with you, and will probably go out of his way to welcome you to your new position. He can do many things to make your orientation into the new position a smoother and more pleasant one than it would otherwise be.

On the other hand, if there was a chronic, continuing

strain between you and one of your new peers when he was over you, he may present an inimical barrier to your initiation into the fraternity, and this man or woman can do as many little mean, sneaky things to put roadblocks in your way as the other former boss does nice ones. Your cue is to be alert for the signals they send, and to interpret them as objectively as you can in your strange surroundings.

The principal thing to remember is that, once you have made your assessment of the attitudes of your peer group, you cannot assume that the climate will be set in concrete for even a few days. There are too many intervening variables present for the situation to remain static.

There are, however, some general precepts you can follow that will be a big help to you in creating overall good relationships between you and your peers. First, maintain generally an optimistic frame of mind. *Expect* your peers to be men of good will, and the majority of them will be. Let's reinforce the fundamental truth that we usually respond in like manner to the way others approach us.

Second, go out of your way to *demonstrate* your own positive frame of mind by being ready with some of the little amenities that make our business life easier. Lend a hand when one of your associates is plowed under. Maybe one of your people could be put on temporary loan to him for a day or so without undue disruption to your operations. If your two groups interlock in any way in the overall departmental job, be sure that your part of the job is never so late as to cause him delays. Share with him information that you think could be of value to his work. Actively seek out ways to be of help.

Third, take care that your lateral communication channels

are always clean, crisp, and concise—yet complete. This can do more to enhance your reputation with your peers than any one thing in the book. We all know how frustrated and angry we get when we discover that we have been left out of a communication chain to our detriment. At the same time, we must not infer that the only sin in communication is that of omission. You can be an irritant in everyone's life if you turn into a consistent overcommunicator. The final outcome of this would be that all your peers would tune you out every time you communicated with them, and would then miss the important as well as the trivial items.

Fourth, remember the overwhelming importance of intellectual honesty in all your peer contacts. Of course, any overt, blatant dishonesty will generally be discovered almost at once and will ring down the final curtain on a managerial career. But there is a more subtle connotation here we must not miss. Deliberate "misunderstandings" of others also constitute intellectual dishonesty. So does the failure to transmit necessary information. So does an ever-so-delicate twisting of the interpretations we give to others of a peer's actions or talk. Try making a list of the ways in which a manager can be intellectually dishonest in his peer dealings under the false assumption that he is helping himself. Your equals are in all probability at least as sharp as you are, and it isn't going to take them forever to uncover any hidden agenda you may be carrying. Once branded as dishonest, you are virtually a dead duck in your peer group.

Fifth, don't expect too much in the way of active friendship from your peers—but, conversely, don't be hyperactive in looking for enmity. After all, you are in a work situation, and all that is ever required of our interpersonal relations in this surrounding is a sum total of interactions that will enable us to achieve our objectives as quickly and economically as possible. Any manager who conceives of his job as a popularity contest is in for a rude awakening.

You will be most successful if you take the attitude that the greatest responsibility for your acceptance or rejection by your associates rests on your shoulders. In other words, keep your frame of mind positive at all times when you are in contact with those on your level. They have problems entirely analogous to yours; help them out by not making them go out of their way to make your relationships smooth.

One word of caution. This book does concentrate entirely on our relationships with others, but we should not fall into the grievous error of assuming that this is the sum total of our managerial responsibility. Most certainly, this is *not* the case. There are many case histories of eminently successful managers whose interpersonal relationships were resoundingly abrasive. True, these managers are in a minute minority, but it can happen. Our job here is to keep in proper perspective the degree to which good relationships can help us in getting the total job done. It is purely and simply one of the best tools for maintaining good balance in our managerial careers. If this thought is always active in our minds, our chances for total success will be multiplied many times.

The Colleague Relationship

The evolution of our modern technology has sired a son not known before on the American management scene. In the younger days of American business and industry, peer relationships among first-line supervisors were of an earthy, intensely pragmatic nature. Foremen tended to stand together in cohesive groups against all other employees: labor on the one hand, and the rest of management on the other. They felt, rightly or wrongly, that they were arrayed against the rest of the world. Now, with the immensely greater technical knowledge required of management at all levels, and with the utilization of many kinds of professionals for many different kinds of work, we are seeing frequent incidence of a colleague relationship, both between the manager and those he supervises, and among managers at different levels.

This is good, for several reasons. First, two or more managers can consider themselves colleagues only when there is true mutual respect expressed among them. This includes both respect for technical expertise and respect for the colleague as an individual. This mutual feeling lays the perfect groundwork for smooth interpersonal relationships on the job.

Second, emergent professionalism has brought with it more cooperation among colleagues than was ever the case before the appearance of this phenomenon. The true professional in any field stands constantly ready to aid and abet any colleague in problem solving, evaluation of ideas, development of methodology, and appraisal of results. This is done in the full knowledge that individual "credit" for results obtained will be blurred—perhaps even lost entirely—in what has become a group effort.

Third, any criticism that may appear will be completely impersonal. It will be leveled against the *process* rather than against the *person* involved in the activity. The manager with this mental set is concerned with what went wrong, rather than with who did wrong. The result is a reduction of abrasive relationships that may harden into active enmities among two or more managers.

Fourth, observance of the colleague relationship among managers can only result in increased respect from those supervised. We all tend to stand a little in awe of the doctor or lawyer of our choice; this same type of feeling will appear in the members of the work group if they see their leadership acting in a truly professional manner. Note that this does not imply a subservient or "master and slave" relationship, but one of true mutual respect and confidence.

Fifth, development of increasingly strong colleague feelings among peers in management will have a fallout of greater productivity in the groups affected. If the manager significantly reduces his attitude of "what's in it for me?", his people will tend to respond with greater effort, less friction, and more attention to the achievement of group goals.

Sixth, increasing self-respect will result in radically improved quality of production. It will be possible to regenerate the pride in craftsmanship so notably absent from the last few generations of our workforce. We have seen this demonstrated in the Japanese working people since the end of World War II. Before that time, a "Made in Japan" label on a product automatically branded it as shoddy and cheap. Today, Japanese lenses, electronic products, and steel products are among the finest in the world. The Japanese are competing with us in these industries on our own terms and are, sad to relate, beating us at our own game.

As can be seen from the foregoing, a colleague relationship among two or more managers is the product of a state of mind more than any other one thing. We must discipline ourselves to make value judgments according to professional criteria, rather than selfish or personal ones. Such a change will require an almost complete readjustment of our thinking, so hard work will be involved in its care and tending during

48

growth. There will be times when we will despair of ever achieving the objectivity which is a prerequisite to this new state of mind. Our cue here is to be impervious to this feeling and forge ahead at all costs to our personal feelings in the matter.

I have made the assertion before in these pages that American management has not yet achieved the state of a true profession. However, the appearance and increase of colleague relationships among significant numbers of managers means that we have made the first critical movement toward arriving at professionalism. It is a sine qua non for that desirable condition. The managerial function of planning must be put to good use by any manager who wants to become a professional. I am talking about his personal planning for his own self-development over a period of years. This is not a state that can be arrived at by a week from next Tuesday by taking a "cram" course, or by reading a couple of good books. Counseling should be sought, and followed, from older and wiser heads in the management field, or from younger and wiser heads as represented by some of the sharp, well-trained young professionals now active in the field of organizational and management development.

Essentially, there is nothing esoteric or difficult about the concept of professionalism. The tools of professional managership are there; it is the manager's responsibility to learn how to use them and to make them his own, so that they will be functional in his work. The hard work comes in practicing until he has truly mastered these tools and uses them automatically. As they become conditioned reflexes, he can then turn his full attention to the job and the problems at hand, and not worry about the mechanisms for solving them.

It would be naive of us to expect that all managers will

assume this posture either willingly or at once. Too much hard labor and mental reorientation are involved for this to occur. Like any other truly good objective, the road to its achievement will be a rocky one, and our shoes will be worn before we get there.

COMPETITION AND INTERPERSONAL RELATIONSHIPS

Whether we like to admit it or not, competition in management land is much more severe and unremitting than in the lower echelons of the workforce. In fact, in some cases it is this competition that attracts candidates to management, and these people are not happy unless they are striving against the efforts of their peers for the achievement of a particular prize.

First, let us establish the fact that there *can* be friendly rivalry. Some people find it possible to enter a game or a race wanting to win, yes, but retaining sufficient self-control to keep their emotions at a manageable level during the course of the contest. This is, of course, the ideal situation, since it allows the job to get done without permanent disruption of relationships that have taken years to build. We say these persons lack the "killer instinct," and it is demonstrable that they do not often scale to the same dizzy heights that some of their competitors do. To them, winning is not everything, and they will settle for less power and prestige for the sake of maintaining their friendships and good relationships with peers. These relatively uncompetitive people can, in their own way, make just as great a contribution to the enterprise as some of the more hagridden members of the management team.

The people who finally rise to the summit of the organization, however, will in nearly every case be highly power-oriented in their personal thinking. We certainly should not be guilty of the simplistic assumption that it is impossible for a man of good will to become the chief of an organization, but these situations are notable for their rarity. Athletes will tell you that they don't become champions without considerable sacrifice of their personal comforts and of other important aspects of their private lives. Similarly, the winner in management competition will have to give up several things that the more ordinary person finds high on his list of values. For example, such a manager may find that the relationships within his family are becoming strained or stunted. The driving young executive may discover he doesn't have the time to spend with his wife and children that he would otherwise deem desirable. Or, for reason of the same time constraints, he or she may discover that old and valued friendships are losing their fine edge, or are dissolving completely. Relations may seem amicable enough on the surface, but when it seems that the old warmth is simply no longer there, it is a sign that formerly strong ties are being severed.

There is a middle ground between these two extremes that many managers find to be functional, both for their own needs and for those of the organization. This is to find a balance between the drive of ambition and extreme damage to interpersonal relationships. The methods for achieving this are relatively simple, at least in theory. Before taking a step designed to promote your own interests, examine minutely the effect it will have on those with whom you associate. Who is likely to be hurt by your proposed course of action? How great will the damage be? Will the advantage accruing to you from it be worth your losses in human contacts?

From time to time, it will be necessary for you to make a calculated decision as to whether you want to, or can afford to, incur the lasting enmity of one of your peers by taking a certain action. It would be childishly naive to assume that any person can ever arrive at a post of eminence in management without having made some enemies. The question is whether you are going to exercise some control over which individuals (and how many) will be added to the list of those actively working against you.

Happily, worsened relationships do not necessarily stay that way. In many cases it is possible to have strained the bonds of friendship without their final severance, and you may find that a little extra effort and attention on your part will save an overall good relationship.

Group living is an ongoing situation of give and take between the members of the team. What we take from others must be at least balanced by what we give to them. This applies to all the people involved in every move you make. It is this running balance sheet of your interactions that you must keep at least subliminally in your consciousness at all times. The sense of balance and perspective it will give you is an attribute without which no manager can continue to be successful.

As a manager, you must also remember that the personal competition in which you become involved does not remain personal for very long. Your people will also be involved in whatever you do individually as a leader/manager, and in the long run you are having either a good or a bad effect on the reputations and relationships of everyone who works for you. This is the kind of responsibility no person should undertake lightly. You may be prepared to sacrifice some of your own friendships, but what if your people find their circle of friendships disturbed as well by your actions? Here is where soul-searching of the first order is mandatory.

Thus you owe it to your people to be candid with them, if for no other reason than to allow them to prepare themselves mentally for what may be in the offing. Tell them if you suspect that a proposed action of yours may lead to some abrasiveness among several members of the group, or with their friends and peers in other groups. It may be possible for them to take evasive actions that will keep them from being seriously harmed by what you are going to do. You are not necessarily giving them a part in your personal decision making, but at least you are being frank and open about its possible effects. Their respect for you will be the greater, even if they do not like what you have told them.

From the earliest days of our culture, we have built the greatness of our nation on the concept of competitiveness. In spite of the attacks being made on this concept by small groups in our midst, it is unlikely that this way of life will be fundamentally altered in our lifetime. However, it is also true that our business survival will in large measure depend on our keeping this competition on a fair and open basis, with ongoing consideration for the fundamental rights and expectations of those working for and with us. Our peers deserve this much from each of us.

How and When to Cooperate

Any serious examination of our culture, and especially our business and industrial structure, will show immediately that it is built on a basis of mutual cooperation. Our civilization would come to a screeching halt within a matter of weeks were the cooperation suddenly to stop.

We have already alluded in passing to the cooperation any manager must exhibit repeatedly in order to get the job done and to keep his relationships with his associates in good running order. But we need to take a closer look at this element of the managerial job to get a proper perspective on its possible effects.

First, true cooperation does not occur if it is obvious that the collaborator is motivated too grossly by "what's in it for me?" There must be at least the semblance of altruism if the cooperation is to be recognized as such. There will be many times in your career as a manager when you will be giving help to those who in all probability will never be in a position to return the favor. But this will be balanced by the fact that at times *you* will get aid and comfort from those situated in such a way that you cannot reciprocate either.

Second, you do owe it to yourself to see that your co-operation does not go so far as to be directly harmful to your own operation. If you seriously curtail a project of your group to lend a hand to a colleague, your reputation for good judgment will be put in jeopardy, and rightly so. Balance must be maintained at all times between what you can and cannot afford to do with the manpower available to you.

Third, you will greatly improve your interpersonal relationships if you *offer* cooperation that you see is needed. Don't wait to be asked if it is obvious to you that you are in a position to help a colleague. He may be hesitating to ask because he is afraid of imposing on you. Your brownie points will be multiplied if your assistance is truly and obviously of your own free will.

Fourth, and in balance to the preceding point, you should take care not to make your help too blatantly obvious to the casual observer. Any manager who earns the reputation of being a "do-gooder" among his peers is suspect as a weakling. Your concern should be the relationship between you and the one other person you are helping; it is the business of no one else what has happened in the situation. If the person you have helped is moved to do so, it is up to him or her to spread the news about your contribution to the effort.

Fifth, let your own people know, quietly, why you are involved in your cooperative venture, since they will also undoubtedly be affected. Any extra effort required of them should be voluntary. If you meet serious or ongoing resistance from them, it would be best to drop the matter and wait for a more propitious time to give another manager a boost.

Perhaps the most important consideration of all in the area of cooperative ventures is the psychological effect on yourself. The fact that you are willing to do a thing above and beyond the call of your specific duties is in itself an indication of a positive attitude on your part. The completion of that action will be self-reinforcing and will produce a sense of euphoria most conducive to good work by you and the members of your group.

Even more pertinent is the fact that almost every venture into helping another person will broaden your knowledge of the whole enterprise and will result in your personal growth and development, which should always be a major consideration in doing your job.

Oddly enough, there are those who find it easy to give cooperation but hard to ask for or receive it. This kind of false pride is a personality defect to be corrected immediately if it appears. It is an indication of an overblown ego, in that it implies that you are intrinsically better in every way than your peers and that they have nothing to offer you of any value to your operation. Of course this is patently untrue. When the time comes, as it will, that your task is bigger than your ability to get it done to meet a deadline, you must have no hesitancy in sending up a flare for assistance.

In conclusion, proper cooperative action within the job structure takes self-discipline of the highest order. This extra effort constitutes another of the drains on your total energy bank, and your best efforts are already needed to make the necessary judgments about "go" or "no go" in a given set of circumstances.

You will save effort in the long run by keeping an actual log of those times when you both give and get cooperation. List the elements in the situation that indicated cooperation was called for. Detail the amount of extra effort required from you or, if the action is coming your way, from the other person. Evaluate carefully the final outcome, to determine whether it was worthwhile to have undertaken or requested the cooperation given. This data bank will prove invaluable to you as it grows over the years. Patterns will evolve that will help you tremendously in making decisions about when to give or get extra help to get the job done. As indicated before, no small part of this analytical process will be determining the motivation behind the request. If the person asking is simply too lazy to do his own work, you could hardly justify extra effort from your group. If, on the other hand, you know this peer to be a normally decent, industrious manager, your first impulse should be to see if it is possible to give him some help.

It should be noted here that the rise and growth of the matrix organization in our business structure will multiply many times the demands for cooperative behavior among managers. (I will have more to say about this in a later chapter.) It is a function of the matrix structure itself that much cooperation be given and received if the structure is to succeed—and in many areas of our modern technology, this is the only viable kind of organization. If a manager has already had trouble in adjusting to demands for cooperation, he will have a horrible time if he finds himself in a matrix. Better to cultivate cooperativeness now than to find ourselves in trouble later.

Changing Relationships

One thing you can be sure of as a manager is that the total picture of your peer relationships will not remain static for many days at a time. The mixture is too yeasty for it ever to set. Vectors going one way today can reverse their direction tomorrow if conditions are altered even slightly.

Some of your more lasting peer relationships will be the result of the political alliances you make in your business career. Whether you like the idea or not, as a successful manager you will be involved to a greater or lesser degree in company politics. You can't survive, let alone advance, unless you make some closely calculated decisions about which of your associates are the comers and enter into some lasting alliances with them. But these, too, will undergo change over the years. As members of your political group are advanced, or leave the company, or retire, successors will have to be recruited to keep your informal organization functional. The struggle for advantage—for power—within any live organization is unceasing, and part of being a manager is recognizing this fact of life.

Other changes in peer relationships are the fallout of organizational changes, especially those that involve a shuffling and reallocation of the available managerial workforce. Enterprises that operate under the project type of organization are especially prone to sudden and frequent realignments of this kind. The completion of one project and the phasing in of another will ordinarily see many alterations of the pyramidal structure. It is possible for a single spectacular success on one project to make a given manager jet-propelled, so that he finds himself operating in nearly a totally new group of peers. In businesses characterized by this sort of "suddenness," peer relationships tend to be shallower and more transitory than they are in more settled and lasting organizational structures.

Peer group relationships are also strongly responsive to changes in the status of the members. Here we mean the status the members have "earned" within the group, not the "imposed" status of nominal position in the hierarchy. As a manager earns more and more respect from his peers by continued solid performance, he can expect that his interpersonal relationships will become easier and more pleasant. In more than a majority of cases, we tend to like those whom we respect. Of course, if there has to be a choice between the two the manager must opt for respect.

Finally, our differential rates of growth and development as managers will have many side effects on peer relationships. In a group of equals, if one or two show much quicker maturation than their fellows, they will actually grow away from their old associates even if such is not their intent. This is not a matter of ill will, in most cases, but simply the result of changing values and broadened perspectives that no longer match those of their associates. It is possible to maintain decent relationships with these former intimates, but the old patina is gone, probably forever.

The entire matter of achieving and maintaining good peer relationships is enormously complex, because of the many independent variables involved. People change, situations change, organizations change, personal motivations change, performances change, pure and simple luck can change. And when we consider that several of these factors can be altering simultaneously, we can see at once the difficulty of maintaining viable relationships with all our associates.

The key to getting and keeping good relationships with our peers is to remain flexible. At all costs, we must be ready to adjust almost instantaneously to the different scenes that will inevitably appear tomorrow. Abraham Maslow, in his humanistic approach to psychology, tells us that the man or woman who enjoys good mental health is the person who operates at the self-actualization level. If we regard our work as an opportunity for continuing personal growth and development, this is bound to result in bettered relationships with our peers.

CHAPTER IV

INTERACTING WITH CUSTOMERS

EVERY MANAGEMENT PERSON will have many and varied contacts with the customers of his enterprise, whether it offers a product or a service to the public. (Though people in the sales department of any company or agency are specialists in the art of selling, they will actually seldom come close to making a majority of the contacts with the receivers of the company's services.) In fact, a manager's general effectiveness will be significantly dependent on his or her ability to interact with the customers in such a way that good relationships will grow and strengthen over the years.

BUILDING THE FOUNDATION

Once the vendor–customer linkage has been effected, similar functions or disciplines in the two enterprises will tend to seek each other out. Members of the customer's engineering department, when they have questions concerning the technical aspects of a product, will soon be bypassing sales to talk with the vendor's engineers. If it is a maintenance type of product or service, the two maintenance departments will gravitate together. A department manager in the customer company will tend to seek out his opposite number in the vendor's organization, since there is a good chance he will know him through professional or trade associations.

Although the fact is obvious, I should still point out that first contacts between managers in the two organizations are critical, they can be "make or break" for the entire life of the relationship. When with prospective or new customers, the manager must exercise the greatest sensitivity. Every cue must be instantly and correctly identified if success is to be assured.

There are a number of important points to observe in making this initial contact. First, it is imperative that the manager who has something to sell makes certain that he has correctly identified and assessed the prospect's needs. We can be *too* expert in our own field and product. If we err by assuming that the customer has greater sophistication than he actually does, the chances are overwhelming that we will botch the deal. At this point, a delicate situation can arise. You, the manager, must be prepared to dig until you have differentiated between true customer *needs* and their *wants*. The two may not be identical in every case. If your careful analysis has told you inescapably that what the customer wants is *not* what he needs, you will be doing him your first great service by pointing this out in your most tactful manner. Once the prospect has been convinced that this is true, you may find that you have lost the sale, but it is almost certain that you will have made a lasting friend. He'll be back another day when you can sell him something he both wants and needs.

Second, your next initial service to your prospect is to make certain that he has a thorough understanding and knowledge of your product. Once again, it is fatal to make any

61

assumptions about his sophistication; you should establish to your own total satisfaction that he is aware of what your product or service can and cannot be expected to do. Take whatever time and pains are necessary to establish this understanding beyond any possible doubt. If he has come to you for a widget and you make framisses, he should learn this as expeditiously as possible.

Third, in the early stages of the relationship it is essential that you clarify what your future responsibilities are concerning your product and your sale. Nowhere is this more clearly illustrated than in the automobile industry. We have seen the pendulum swing wildly in the past few years with regard to manufacturers' guarantees on new cars. From "12 months and 12,000" to "5 months and 50,000" and back again has been the cycle. No manager should ever allow himself to jeopardize his company's total reputation by ignoring one "lemon"—either product or service—that might prejudice the customer against him forever. Properly established delimitations of future warranties and service responsibilities are the only safeguard you have against this eventuality. It is your responsibility to communicate thoroughly in this area.

Fourth, the alert manager will make an early assessment of the nature of the personal (or impersonal) relationship that the prospective customer desires with the vendor. Are you expected to socialize to a certain extent, or is this a "no-no"? In the former situation, you are under peril of having impossible demands made on you; the latter case may result in a sterile kind of relationship that will not be as fully productive as you might wish. Usually you should seek a happy medium that will give both partners in the relationship a little latitude of movement.

Fifth, in this same connection, make certain that you do not appear to be applying pressure at any point in the young relationship. All of us instinctively recoil from the blatantly obvious "hard sell." This is not to say that you cannot be persistent, but do so in a low-keyed, unobtrusive sort of way that will put no blips on his personal radar.

These points are, of course, generalizations of the broadest kind. There is no set formula for instant success in corralling a new customer; if there were, selling would immediately lose its challenge and the opulent rewards it now offers to the expert. Once again, we are calling on the manager to use his native good sense and judgment to weigh and evaluate each situation according to its individual characteristics. Your good judgment will have to tell you which type of approach to choose for each new contact made. The time you will have in which to make this decision will be traumatically short; in some situations, the decision will have to be intuitive rather than coldly logical or well documented.

The thing to remember is that you carry the future of your enterprise in your hands every time you make a first encounter with a prospective customer. This knowledge alone should be sufficient to elicit your best efforts and complete concentration of your powers of analysis and judgment. One thing is certain: You are dealing with other human beings, and they are subject to the same sorts of misgivings that you are feeling at this time. You are in at least as good a position as he is, if your product is worthy of your dedication and efforts. At the risk of sounding like a cracked record, I will point out that this is another situation where you could choose no better course than to keep a written record of what occurs in your first encounters with the prospect.

PUTTING UP THE SUPERSTRUCTURE

Many managers feel that once the delicate job of establishing the vendor–customer relationship has been accomplished, it will be self-perpetuating. Nothing could be further from the truth.

The principal danger, of course, is that the vendor manager will start to take the customer for granted. He may assume that since the orders are coming in regularly he no longer needs to spend significant amounts of time on maintaining the relationship. If the customer begins to feel neglected, the scene can get pretty messy. The first thing he will do is to put out feelers for a new source contact—or several. This action will result in a rather close scrutiny of your enterprise's methods (and products) as compared to the others being examined.

Maintaining an ongoing relationship between you and the customer is a positive kind of action. Regularity of contact is a must, yet you should be careful not to become a drain on their business time. One thing you should do routinely is to broaden your number of contacts within the customer organization. Never rely solely on a personal relationship with one of their employees. He may leave, retire, be promoted, or in some other way be removed as the key person in the relationship. As you visit the customer, or have any sort of contact with them, make positive efforts to meet the peers of your original contact and get them into the arena of interface. The more people in the customer organization who know you as "the" representative of the vendor, the better will be your chances of carrying on smoothly over a long period of time.

Next, be sure that you keep on top of significant changes

in the customer's situation. How is his business? Is the company growing? How do his products or services compare with those of his competitors? Most certainly, you should read their house organs and their annual report with close attention.

As your relationship with the customer matures, it becomes increasingly important that you give periodic evidence of being willing to go out of your way to give special service to the account. Volunteer your services; don't wait for them to find it necessary to ask you for these favors. It is not necessary that these be major—their size is not as critical as the fact that they evidence your good will and show that you value the relationship.

You must also do continuous monitoring to reassure yourself that you are remaining competitive. While it is true that with solid vendor–customer relationships, minor price differentials will usually not result in losing the account, you must still make certain that your operation remains such that you can avoid large and fatal underbidding by a new competitor. Thus as a manager you must be literate in at least two industries: yours and theirs. And, in turn, you must relate your knowledge to the movements of the economy at large.

Another thing you should do is to acquaint yourself with the customer's company policy about gifts and objects of value coming from the vendor. This spectrum is indeed a broad one. Some companies make no bones about the fact that they expect some "cumshaw" from time to time. Others maintain a rigid policy of "hands off." In the latter kind of organization, any attempt to give an item of value will result in immediate termination of your relationship. This danger area extends into the matter of entertainment as well. You need to know whether you can safely take your customer's representative out to lunch or dinner, or whether this would be construed as an effort at bribery. How about the golf course? Some companies give open recognition to the fact that their managers consummate some important business deals in this type of atmosphere; others consider it indicative of a frivolous attitude toward doing business. The data you gather in these areas will be of immense value to you in maintaining the contact that was so carefully begun.

Another excellent way of solidifying the superstructure is to become a source of information for the customer. Share with them the information you pick up from your other contacts—making sure, naturally, that you do not give them any data which could harm your organization. In general, your customers will value you more highly if they get to know you as a source for general business information that is accurate and trustworthy.

You should also make sure that you pass along information which has to do with the "futures" of your orders. If this is the negotiation year for your labor contract and you feel there is a high probability of your being hit with a strike, your customer should know this in time to do his own inventory planning. Or, if there is a major change in layout of process under consideration in your company that might result in some delays in delivery downstream while the changeover is being effected, your customer has a right to know this fact in plenty of time. If you feel that general dissemination of this information would work a hardship on your organization, make sure your customer knows this, and appeal to his integrity not to harm you by his possession of this information. Ninety percent of the time, he will behave honorably toward you. In any event, the successful continuation of your relationship with this customer will partly depend on your ability and willingness to give him the information he needs.

At the same time, it should be made clear to the vendor that you consider this a reciprocal arrangement. If you are willing to be cooperative in this area, so must he.

If the process of building a strong and lasting relationship with a customer begins to give you some of the sensations of a tightrope walker in a circus, join the club. It is a course loaded with many booby traps and obstacles, but if they weren't there, where would the challenge be?

How Much Can You Be Imposed On?

It is an unfortunate fact of life that "old" or "preferred" customers may come to presume on the relationship between you. Of course, the preference they assume may be entirely a product of their imagination; you may be trying desperately to treat them just the same as any other client.

Actually, your own actions in establishing and building the relationship would tend to give a semblance of truth to their assumptions. You have gone out of your way to be accommodating; you have made special efforts to learn about their company and their industry; you have broadened your acquaintanceship among their personnel deliberately—all of these things having been done in a real effort to build a lasting connection between you and them.

So what kind of a balancing act can you perform to keep from getting into a situation where they will presume upon their "special" place?

You should first let them know your company policy on this matter, which will naturally state that all customers are to receive the same treatment. If you are careful, this can be done smoothly and unobtrusively sometime early in your meetings, when you are mutually exploring your two organizations. Chances are heavily in favor of their having a very similar statement in their own policy book, and they will know this is really the only fair way to operate.

There will inevitably come the time (or times) when they will request—or demand—that special priority be given to the delivery of their orders. This is the most dangerous kind of imposition, and the most frequent one you will meet. An emergency will always be claimed, and their documentation may even be convincing. Your only recourse here is to study each of these instances as an individual case, and let it be known that whatever decision is reached, it will not constitute a precedent. If it is in the cards for you to give them an earlier date, *without harming another customer*, what's the difference if you do? The categorical imperative here is communication with all parties concerned. Perhaps one of your other customers would just as soon take a little delay, especially if his order was simply for inventory stockpiling. But never delay anyone's order for any reason without informing him of what is going to happen. At the same time, impress on the one for whom you're doing the favor that this must not be habit forming; it cannot be allowed to become a way of life with him, for the good of both your organizations.

Another, and most irritating, gambit of old customers is to approach you for such personal favors as getting hard-to-come-by tickets for the theater or athletic events. This is one of those cases where you will probably grit your teeth and get them for him if you have the connections. He has no right to make this sort of request; he knows it, and you know it. But he probably will, since he is a human being, and while he is doing it he will rationalize by saying that it has nothing to do with business at all. You are a good friend of his and he "would do the same for you."

One of the touchiest situations arises when your valued customer asks you for private information about a mutual friend or acquaintance. It may be that the person is being considered for employment by the customer firm and that the customer wants information which is not really germane to the hiring situation. If there is ever a time when a lie is justified, this is it. Claim, in all bland innocence, that you don't know anything about what he is after. He may or may not believe you, but there is nothing he can do about this and retain any semblance of decency. If he does turn away from you, he's not the kind of account you would really want in the long run anyway.

The mental set you need here is continuous monitoring of your own professional attitude. If you really have it, there will be little necessity to verbalize about it. Your customers will recognize it in you, and will respect you the more for it. However, with a certain kind of person who doesn't recognize an old pro when he sees one, there is another ploy that will sometimes work. That is to turn his own methodology back on him. Use the same tactics with him that he has been employing on you. Unless he is definitely mentally retarded, he'll get the message pretty quickly and will mend his ways, perhaps going so far as to joke with you about the subject. Some of the more lovable scoundrels get a kick out of being discovered.

But, on balance, you will have to learn to live with a certain amount of imposition from all of your customers from time to time. It should be noted that this inherently occurs more often in the service industries than in the manufacturing or product industries. If you are in business to give service, it will become increasingly difficult for your customers to differentiate between legitimate and illegitimate demands on your time and efforts.

Above all, don't hesitate to send up a flare for help when you find yourself trapped. Tell your superiors what is going on. Maybe they can conveniently manufacture a new directive from mahogany row that will take you off the hook. Perhaps a word from one of your executives to his opposite number in the customer organization will get the word down the line to the offender in a way that will allow him to save face before you, and this is important to your ongoing relationship. Maintaining self-respect is gravely important to us all; we should remember this in our business relationships as well as our personal ones.

On the personal side, the general state of your health and level of energy will be one of the greatest determinants of your ability to bear up under these continuing pressures. Scientists have clearly demonstrated that reactions to stress situations are positively correlated to the level of physical well-being. Internal organizational pressures are more easily borne than those imposed upon us from the outside; we know that if necessary we can have a showdown with those in our own group without the danger of losing revenue that is vital to the firm's success. Perhaps your annual physical should become semiannual. And, for goodness sake, keep your domestic fences mended, so that family problems don't make the mélange totally insupportable!

Customers' Organizational Changes

It is inevitable that there will be personnel changes in the customer organization which will have an effect on you, the vendor company. The people with whom you have been doing most of your interacting will leave, be promoted, be transferred—in other words, your contact will be a new person. While it is true that inertia will tend to carry along the interaction between the two organizations without a serious breach, it is also true that the change presents some danger to the continuity of your sales to them.

First, the new representative responsible for the procurement of your product or service may have some favorite vendor of his own to whom he will want to change the account. You must probe this possibility immediately, but delicately, as soon as the change has been announced. You may decide that the best approach is the open one: asking him directly whether he intends to continue buying your products at the same rate as in the past. His answer to this will naturally determine your course of action. If he says yes, you have, in effect, an entire reselling job to do with him to prevent a switch. It is mandatory that you have at your fingertips all pertinent data, both about the product itself and about the service record your company has built up over the years in your vendor role. Make it appear to him that a change would be so illogical that he would have difficulty in defending such an action to his own people. It goes without saying that this can be done only if your record with them has been impeccable.

Your interface with the customer can also be seriously affected when an executive at policy-making level, with whom you ordinarily have little contact, is replaced by another person whose beliefs and business philosophy are at wide variance with those of the former incumbent. For example, the new executive may reexamine the original "make or buy" decision made many years ago. He may decide that it will be cheaper or more effective for his company to manufacture your product themselves, which of course will leave you out of the picture.

This is your signal to convey the danger to your executives, and they must move into the action at once to see whether it is possible to forestall this change. Your job here is to see that the executives involved are perfectly prepared with all the data they will need to defend your position.

There is another sort of change, not necessarily involving different personnel, that is occurring more and more frequently and can have a strong effect on your position as a vendor. Many organizations that historically have been strongly centralized in their operations are finding it expedient to restructure on a project basis, especially if they are in a technical, engineering, or scientific field. This has a tendency to splinter their purchasing function, since each project group created will have responsibility for every management and operational discipline necessary to complete the project. You may suddenly discover that to remain in competition you will have to build and maintain not one but several contacts in the same company in order to keep all your business with them. If you are alert to the possibilities, this change might result in *more* sales to this customer than ever before, since each project group will tend to maintain its own inventory of necessary parts and components. This characteristic is one of the questionable aspects of project organization for a company, but it may work out to your advantage if you play your cards carefully.

One ever present danger you must watch for is the possibility of power struggles developing between peers in the customer's organization. This is always bad for the enterprise involved, but your concern is that it endangers your position as a vendor until the struggle has been resolved. One of the divisive points in the fight may be the source of procurement for necessary materials. If your ally loses the war, you will probably be a casualty so far as continuing as their source of supply is concerned. The winner will make a change. However, even though this possibility may loom large, it is a terrible mistake for you to involve yourself directly in the struggle. Your neutrality should be complete and perfectly self-evident to any observer. Once you have committed yourself to either side, you have passed the point of no return.

These are some of the more cogent reasons for maintaining many points of contact with your customer's personnel. Your intelligence reports must be as complete as possible for you to remain competitive in the ebb and flow of the action within the customer organization. Your principal hope is that you will be forewarned of impending changes in time to map strategies for coping with them. This is some of the most important managerial planning you will ever do, and the more alternatives you think of and plan for, the greater will be your chances of survival as the favored vendor. That you remain flexible and agile in the relationship is imperative.

It is obvious from this discussion that there is an inherent and ongoing symbiosis between the "thing" decisions you make and the personnel involved in the action. In making your decisions about the thing situations, you will be giving more attention to "people" considerations in your vendor role than when the decision only affects your own organization. This is true because you have more control over your personnel than you have over your customer's. In any situation, much more persuasive pressure can be put on your people than on outsiders.

Flux and significant change are a continuing part of the American industrial scene. They will increase rather than decrease in the foreseeable future, and we must prepare ourselves mentally to live with this condition from here on out.

There is an obvious corollary to this that should not be overlooked. Major changes in *our* organization will have an impact on our dealings with our customers in exactly the same way that their changes affect us. As a change becomes imminent, you must prepare a course of action that will neutralize any possible bad effects on your customer–vendor roles. You may just be the only person in your enterprise who can save the customer, and your actions will be crucial in this kind of emergency.

Building for the Future

In the managerial jungle we get so used to fighting today's skirmishes and putting out today's fires that we may forget to plan properly for our future activities. Vendor–customer relationships, to be really viable, should be ongoing. The longer they last, the easier and smoother becomes the relationship, resulting in increased efficiencies for both enterprises.

How can we best assure that we will maintain good relationships with our customers? There are some musts that we cannot afford to overlook; they comprise the backbone of the entire relationship. Some of them have already been mentioned in other contexts, but they should be reinforced here for the sake of proper perspective.

First: Above all else, keep the channels of communication open both ways. Each of the organizations concerned has a need to know certain things about the other; each has the responsibility of sending along information necessary to the other. Is there a danger that the flow of some of your ingredients or components may be interrupted? Your customer should be apprised of this fact, so that he can make his plans for inventory control without undue time pressure. Does he expect unusually heavy sales during a time of year when business is usually slack? He owes you this information so that you can gear up for an extra effort at the right time.

Second (and this, too, is in the communication vein): keep your customer reasonably up to date on the state of the art in your industry. He has some responsibility of his own in this area, but the heaviest onus will be on you to let him know what to expect as far ahead as you yourself can see. Are you in electronics? Let your customer know, if he doesn't already, the probable impact of photoelectronics on both your business and his. It may have a major effect on his company's product line or sales efforts. He will certainly be grateful for any advance notice he can get from you about new developments that touch both your businesses.

Third: Let the human elements in the relationships of your two firms develop naturally. Don't try to force them in a certain direction; to do so will make your customer feel uneasy and threatened. If it is in the cards that you and your contact are to become close personal friends over the years, so be it. If it seems more natural that your interface remain on a purely business basis, you can assume that is the way it was meant to be. By the same token, let the same natural course of events control your relationships with the entire network of people you have come to know in the customer's organization. Your degree of personal closeness with them will, and should, vary widely.

Fourth: Go out of your way to foster a "clubby" atmosphere in your relationships with the customer. Make it a subtle honor to be one of the insiders among the business associates in the two organizations. It is your job to create good memories of the events that have occurred between you over the years, and you should respond visibly to their efforts to maintain the best of interactions.

To recapitulate, this chapter has been concerned with a cyclical kind of relationship that ordinarily grows between vendor and customer. The cautious first steps are calculated to build a solid base on which an enduring entente can be built. Once the general tenor has been established as warm and open, you must at all costs avoid the danger of taking the customer for granted—or even letting him think that such is happening. More solid effort goes into this second stage than the first maneuverings. Some basic decisions must be made early, and communicated delicately, as to how far you are willing to be imposed on by the customer, and in what areas. You must make careful plans for the organizational changes that will inevitably occur in the customer concern. The important thing is not to be caught off balance; you should plan for enough alternatives so that you will never be at a loss for a counter move. Simultaneously with all of these events, you will have to be planning for the future of the relationship between your two enterprises, in both thing and people areas. Change is a way of life in our technology; you as a manager must become accustomed to this climate and respond viably to its pressures and traumas.

CHAPTER V

INTERACTING WITH VENDORS

IN THIS CHAPTER you will be making another of the many role-reversals American businessmen face in their work life. The preceding chapter was concerned with our relationships with customers; this one will examine how we relate to the vendors who furnish us with our raw materials or subassemblies. Some of the differences in these two situations are gross; some are subtle and hard to distinguish.

How Does the Vendor Differ from the Customer?

The most obvious answer to this question (but not always a true one) is that he is the asking party, just as you are when you approach your customer. He has something of value to contribute to your product or service, but in almost every case he faces competition in varying degrees from other enterprises in the same business. This fact alone tends to put you on the defensive—on guard—in your initial contacts with his representative. There is enough of the Yankee trader in all of us to entertain a few suspicions at first of the "drummer" who knocks on our door. This is true even if we go looking for him in the Yellow Pages or a directory of manufacturers.

Next, and of great importance to your getting acquainted, it is probable that he knows more about your concern than you do about his, at least if he is at all well informed on his market potential. It is perfectly possible that he will be able to tell you things about your company you weren't aware of yourself! Remember that a few pages back I pointed out the necessity of your knowing all you could discover about your potential new customer before planning your sales campaign. Your vendors will most likely have done this preliminary study of *you* at some time or another.

The vendor, if he anticipates that the relationship will be a continuing one, has a vested interest in the success of your business, whereas your customer doesn't. The customer can find your product elsewhere, while the vendor will depend on continuing sales to you for his production continuity. This is the basic reason why it is easier to establish and maintain good relations with a vendor than with a customer. He can't afford to see you fail. This fact will color your interfacing to a remarkable degree. You have every right to expect him to be attentive to your needs and desires, because a successful and smooth relationship is of great importance to both of you. To put it baldly, you are above him in the pecking order.

One special situation should be considered, however. This is the case in which you are dealing with a monopoly, such as a utility. In the past, some monopolies have had notoriously bad relationships with their customers simply because they knew the customer *had* to come to them. It should be noted, however, that this scene is changing rapidly these days. A more enlightened and sophisticated general public is starting to demand things of the monopolies that they wouldn't have thought of a generation ago. A good example can be found in the history of the American aluminum industry from its inception until the year 1958. At first one company alone, then a second and a third, maintained what amounted to a monopoly on the supply of this useful light metal. Customers came with hat in hand, literally begging to get supplies necessary for the fabrication of their aluminum products. The job of the aluminum "salesmen" was reduced to that of an order taker, with perhaps a tinge of trying to placate those who were low on the priority list. The recession of 1958 reversed this overnight, and permanently. For the first time, the business became highly competitive, since coincidental with the economic setback huge new quantities of production capacity came on-stream. The readjustment in the thinking of managers in the aluminum industry was traumatic in the extreme—and hilarious to watch, if one wanted to be snide about the matter.

But, as we know, cases of monopoly are in a very small minority, and for the most part the vendor knows he has to toe a special line to keep his business with you. But that doesn't mean you can just relax; it is important that you make a real effort at maintaining wholesome relationships from your side of the interaction. There are many times when the vendor literally holds in his hands the life of our organization, and we should always remember this. There is bound to come a time when his delivery of needed materials will be critical to your meeting your deadlines, and that is make or break for you.

The vendor differs from the customer in another special way: In essence, the quality of your product can be no better than the quality of the component he furnishes you. Later in this chapter the matter of his quality-control effort will be considered in more detail; the subject is just mentioned here for the sake of perspective.

Since, then, the mental set of your vendor is quite different from that of your customer, you must make readjustments in your thinking about him and your approaches to him. He wants to please you, yet you can't afford to be whimsical or arbitrary in your treatment of him, since at some crucial time your existence will depend on his probity and good will. In only a generic way are you his "patron," and certainly you can't afford to be patronizing to him. He has the same feelings and sensitivities you have, and deserves the same consideration you give to others you relate to.

Perhaps at this point we could benefit from giving a moment's thought to the changeability of the vendor–customer relationship and the emergence of the matrix type of organization on the American industrial scene. The more complex our culture becomes, the more shifting and fluid are our roles and relationships. One moment we are the "boss," while a few minutes later we become the subordinate, *and perhaps in contact with the same person.* Moreover, we are gradually coming to realize that our responsibilities as managers are not only to the organization as a whole, or to the industry as an entity, but to the entire economy—to the public weal, if you will. Our thinking and actions must be conditioned by our value judgments as to their effect on the total scene; it is not enough to just pursue narrow or selfish goals. At this point, and as far as we can see into the future, our responsibility in management far transcends the limits of our own enterprise, no matter how huge it may be. This basic dictum should be the lodestar on which we center the navigation of our entire managerial career. Our concern for international affairs should extend beyond worrying about the convulsions we are currently suffering over the Common Market or the monetary crisis. Our future safety and survival will depend on our conceptualization of a duty to the welfare of the entire world. This is not starry-eyed idealism; it is self-protection of the most basic kind.

How Much Time Do You Give the Vendor?

One of the more delicate aspects of the relationship between customer and vendor is determining how much time will be involved in making and servicing the sales. Naturally, there is going to be a wide variance in this among different kinds of businesses and the different products or services sold. But in every situation there has to be a happy medium for this time involvement, and it is the prerogative of the customer to determine how much of his working day he will allow to a vendor. There are some overall criteria any manager should keep in mind to help him make this decision.

The first is that, for certain, you will want to know everything *necessary* about the product you are buying. Nothing can be more maddening than to discover you have been misusing a part or a subassembly because you didn't know how to service it properly. What kind of preventive maintenance cycle should be followed with a new piece of machinery? Your vendor is in the best position to tell you, and if he doesn't volunteer the information, you should push him for it. It is going to take time for him to tell you the little tricks and gimmicks in the operation of a new item; you can scarcely begrudge him this time, for to do so would be to shortchange yourself. You may have a breakdown because of something you didn't know that he could have told you.

Second, develop a fine intuitive sense of the point at which the vendor starts to "visit" instead of keeping to the business at hand. Not that you want your relationship to be coldly impersonal or without any kind of involvement, but an unconscionable amount of time can be wasted with a vendor if he is trying to work a personality con game on you. If this is a favorite gambit of his, it will probably show up quite early in the relationship, and this is the time to indicate the boundaries once and for all. Better to define the limits now than to wound him more deeply after your relationship grows older and has become set. In the long run, you will both be happier if this is done.

Third, at some time you will surely have to confront the question of whether you will become involved socially off the job. It is difficult to give any guidelines in this case, because it is a personal matter between two individuals. It is analogous to the age-old problem of whether the boss will "fraternize" with his people, and the same decision-making factors are involved. On every manager rests the responsibility of knowing himself well enough to make valid decisions about how far this social interacting can be carried. If there is danger that a growing friendship may becloud the validity of business judgments, you are of course on dangerously thin ice. If, on the other hand, you find it possible to compartmentalize your thinking into business *and* social, and your vendor representative also has this happy faculty, there is no inherent danger in cultivating a personal friendship as far as you wish.

Fourth, it is important to make fine distinctions as to *when* you allot the vendor time with you. You know your schedule better than anyone else; since he is the asker, your decision is always final. If he should call at the time of the quarter when you are deeply involved in production reports, or when you are making a changeover in product lines, or when there is a crisis of any sort, your vendor has no right to feel the least bit slighted if you indicate crisply that his timing is bad. In fact, if you play the "good guy" here and allow him to come in when your better judgment says you don't have the time, the irritation that develops can seriously endanger the whole relationship. You can only assume that he is a reasonable adult and will understand your reasons for being unavailable at a given time or under a specific set of circumstances. In fact, he will respect you the more for this evidence of sound business sense.

Getting to know your vendor well enough to do business with him properly is not necessarily a linear function of the time spent with him. It is more a qualitative than a quantitative matter, and you should evaluate each of your sessions with him in the light of cold, hard reason and on the basis of the results achieved by each interface.

Another consideration cannot be overlooked: It is entirely possible that *you* might be unconsciously guilty of monopolizing too much of *his* time, and this is as unfair to him as when the reverse is true. Remember, he has other customers to whom he has obligations—some of them may be even more important to him than you are, heaven forbid!

Ordinarily, customer and vendor will achieve the best of all possible relationships if they face the time problem squarely and together. Talk it out. Set reasonable limits and then stick to them, recognizing always that special situations may arise at any time which will change the entire picture. In other words, be as flexible here as you pride yourself on being over the entire gamut of your managerial life. This, like any other business relationship in these times, is a cooperative venture, and its success will depend on the full cooperation of both parties and a complete meeting of the minds about the questions involved. You both must recognize that your goals and special interests differ, and must be prepared to adjust your interactions accordingly. If you do this, the matter of time allotment will cease to be a major problem and can be worked out to the best advantage for both of you.

If, as is likely, you have several vendors, you will need to develop a priority list of vendor time allotment. In most cases this is not a difficult decision; it is conditioned by the importance of the purchase to your final product or service. No one can fault you for spending many more hours with your most important vendor than you do with those of lesser value. It is, actually, your particular duty to arrive at this priority·list and then to observe it rigorously. There is no other way to fly!

Putting On the Squeeze

It is inevitable that times will arise in your business when you feel you must put pressure on your vendor for special consideration. Perhaps a customer is asking you for an accelerated delivery date for his orders. Maybe you have taken on some new customers and your working inventory has been depleted. Or there could be danger of a strike in your industry or your customer's, and the only sensible thing to do is to stockpile your products as fast as you can before the trouble starts. There can be many different reasons, all of them valid, for your having to go to your vendor and put the squeeze on him.

Before you do, however, make certain that your "emergency" is a real one, and that you can document this to the vendor irrefutably. Any way you look at it, your request is going to spell trouble for him; if you value your relationship, be sure that you have his complete understanding of and sympathy for your situation. There are some unfortunate souls who make this approach a way of life, and their vendor relationships have a way of deteriorating fast.

Next, be sure that you have done your internal homework well. Is the planning complete for the readjustment of your production schedule? Will the vendor make the extra effort to accede to your demand, only to learn later that his materials were not immediately used and that he had gone the extra mile in vain? If that ever happens, you are in big trouble.

Finally, stay with your vendor during this trying period. Your communications will have to be stepped up significantly if the thing is to work. Be ready to burn a little extra electricity; your days will be longer, and your nights shorter, until the emergency has been licked. So, naturally, will be the days of your vendor representative, and you should be prepared to give him ample recognition for his sacrifice. Make a public ceremony, if necessary, of awarding him the Purple Heart for his wounds. At the very least, it should be routine that you notify his supervisors formally of the fact that he went out of his way to help you. His own communication with his people about the occurrence cannot have the same impact as a word from you that his actions were important. If this leads to a bonus or a raise for him, he isn't likely to hate you for your part in it.

One consideration must never be lost sight of: Every time you go to the vendor with a special request, you must be prepared to give him quid pro quo. The next time he reports to you a possible delay in an order of yours, you should make every effort to accommodate his need. In other words, it has to be a two-way street, and you should view a favor received as a debt incurred.

An analogy can be drawn here: Mutual courtesies in the business world have the same lubricating effect as they do in our personal lives. If in general we are receptive to the idea of exchange of favors, our interpersonal relationships at work will be strengthened just as much as they are at home when this philosophy is followed.

Sometimes a situation arises that calls for an agonizing decision on your part. Say your customer is pressuring you for an early delivery—putting the screws on you mercilessly—and the only way to give him what he wants is to get special consideration from your vendor. But perhaps you have been to the well three or four times in the past year, for different reasons. And maybe you know that this would be the last straw for him, and would seriously inconvenience, or even threaten, his entire operation. In this case you have the unenviable duty of weighing the relative importances of the customer and the vendor. Over the long haul, which of them is going to be more important to you? If you have to make a choice, would the loss of the customer or the loss of the vendor be more critical to your overall operations? If the customer's orders are only a minute part of your gross business, perhaps he is expendable, but what if his business constitutes a significant part of your total gross? Does your vendor sell you a product widely used throughout your product line, or is it a specialty item for only one or two products? Quite probably, at this point you will wisely call for the counsel of your boss and the executive echelon of your organization.

Better to share the responsibility for this decision than to take the blame for something that could turn into a catastrophe whichever way it goes.

Yet, withal, it is a psychological fact of life that we tend to feel friendlier to those people for whom we have performed favors and extra services. That is, if there are reasonably few situations in which your vendor has to extend himself to satisfy you, your overall ties with him will probably be strengthened rather than weakened by these events. After all, we have a personal stake in the recovery of the patient for whom we donated blood, haven't we?

The decisions you make in this area will strongly affect your maturation as a manager, since the results of these decisions will have a visible effect on the health of your operations and the entire organization. Decisions on problems that have only internal effects can sometimes be buried if they are less than perfect; it is next to impossible to evade scrutiny if your decisions have an outside implication, with either vendors or customers.

Monitoring Quality Control

It will be constantly necessary for you to stay on top of the quality of the products your vendor sells you. The fact that he was able to meet your specifications the first time around doesn't take you off the hook with regard to an ongoing monitoring process. The way to keep this process from intruding on and threatening the developing relationship between your two companies is to see that it becomes habitual from the very inception of your business dealings. You, or someone in your organization, should be responsible for sampling and testing every delivery they make to you. Remember the warning about taking your customer for granted—your vendor may do the same with you unless you let him know nicely that he'd better not.

Monitoring quality control is not only a basic of good business practice; it can also be an actual vehicle for strengthening the bonds between you and the vendor. The greater the pile of data that show continuing acceptability, the greater will be the mutual respect between your enterprises. Americans are just as respondent to "old" traditions of quality as are any other national group. We may not have the exact equivalent of "By Appointment to Her Majesty" (the British seal of approval), but the general concept is present.

So, then, how do you deal with the inevitable time when you receive one or more shipments of their goods that are defective? Maybe the variance is so minimal that, by stretching just a bit, you could concede it to be within tolerances, but you just don't like the way the situation has developed. The general answer to this is to keep your complaints low keyed, stay low in the water, and present a low profile. There can be more than a hint of "It happens to all of us, so let's forget it and start all over again next time." Your vendor representative will be appreciative of the fact that you are not ready to hang him from the yardarm because of one tiny slip.

Yet, at the same time, there should be the clear and unmistakable intimation that this must not continue or your doing business together will be endangered. You are completely in the driver's seat; there is no product made or service rendered that can't be duplicated by someone else if they try hard enough, and your vendor knows it.

Another act on your part which will be of great help to him is to indicate your readiness to help him find the cause of the trouble. Has there been a variance or a change in their layout or production methods? Are new personnel (perhaps imperfectly trained) on the line? Has there been a change in their packaging or shipping procedures? And you should be just as ready to look at your side of the coin. Have *you* changed something in your receiving or handling of the materials? What about new personnel in your shop? Or has there been some minor alteration of your production methods that could have some sort of effect on your vendor's product not immediately discernible to the casual observer? The important thing is to make sure that no possible reason for the difficulty goes uninvestigated by either you or your vendor. This is the time for the closest sort of cooperative actions between you.

One aluminum manufacturer (Kaiser Aluminum & Chemical Corporation) changed its source of bauxite, the raw ore from which aluminum is extracted, because the new source was more plentiful, more easily available, and in the long run looked as if it would be a big money saver. The only difficulty was that it was much harder to process into an acceptable grade of alumina, and hundreds of thousands of dollars had to be spent on research and new equipment before the cheaper grade of ore could be made workable to everyone's satisfaction. What had seemed to be a stroke of business genius actually turned out to be a year-long liability of the first magnitude. The fact that the company was its own vendor didn't change anything in the picture. Another division of the company bought, mined, and shipped the bauxite, but to the people in the process plants that produced the alumina, it might just as well have been procured from complete strangers. There were hard feelings for years between the two divisions of the company.

Another caution you, the purchaser, must observe is to keep yourself from becoming a nitpicker. Yes, you are the boss—the customer always is—but remember that there is a broad spectrum of *kinds* of bosses. Some are liked, and some are not. What started on your part as a fairly straightforward running check of your vendor's product quality can deteriorate into a witch hunt unless you are careful to keep things in perspective. The line between being a respected, quality-conscious purchaser and a doddering old fussbudget is sometimes a thin one.

It has been said repeatedly that the greatest casualty of the American production line has been pride in workmanship, and that therefore the maintenance of quality standards has become an inordinately heavy chore. In many cases, this is the plain truth. Your job, then, as a customer and (hopefully) friend of your vendor representative is to keep hammering away at the fact that quality workmanship depends just as much on state of mind as on technical expertise. The best workman in the world can turn out a shoddy product if his mental attitude toward his work deteriorates. This is sometimes more easily detected by the outsider than by a member of the team producing the defective material. If you think this may be a factor in the trouble with your purchase, try to get your vendor to let you come in and observe his plant's or office's operations. You may be able to spot the trouble where he can't, simply because of his long familiarity with the people involved. Changes in morale may have been so gradual and imperceptible that he simply isn't aware of them.

Quality monitoring of your vendor's products requires a careful mix of unyielding standards and a mental attitude that is basically hopeful. You have all the faith and confidence in the world in the good intentions of your vendor; your sole concern is to rectify the trouble, rather than to find a "culprit" at whom to point a finger.

WHEN CAN YOU EXPECT A BREAK?

I spoke already of the times when it may be necessary for you to put pressure on a vendor, and of how these situations can affect your relationship with the seller's representative. But sometimes the situation is reversed, and you will find yourself being offered a break gratuitously by your supplier. Perhaps he will come to you with advance information on a new product which will be important to you and which, if you have it first, will give you a tremendous market advantage over your competitors. Or he may come to you with information about your competitors' actions and movements that you can turn to your advantage.

Naturally, these things will happen only when the best of relationships exist between the two of you. Even though there is business in it for him, there would be anyway if he went to someone else with the information. His coming your way is an indication of his good will and concern for your company's welfare.

Your response to this sort of overture is a delicate thing. Obviously, you should express gratitude—but not too much. Most people are embarrassed when others fawn over them. Play it down the middle, but hint that this is most certainly credit for him in your bank which he can tap anytime in the future. One thing you should certainly do is to keep him apprised of the effect of his action on your business. He will want to know that what he did was of real advantage to you.

Another kind of break you may sometimes get from your vendor occurs, oddly enough, when his own firm is for some reason under pressure. Perhaps their cash flow has dwindled to a trickle, and he has arranged with his sales people to give you a special—and very good—price if you will increase your inventory significantly over the next six months. If your calculations show that carrying more inventory will still yield a higher profit in the long run, both you and the vendor can benefit from this kind of cooperation. It goes without saying that this situation should be thoroughly explained to, and cleared with, your supervisors before final action is taken. Anything less than this falls into the dangerous category of "surprising the boss"!

You may also receive a break from a vendor when another customer of his has made a faux pas and angered him. While he is exercising that quite human trait of seeking revenge, you are getting a chance to benefit yourself. Of course, this sword has two edges. If he will do it to someone else, you yourself might be the next victim of his reaction to personal pique. Handle this one with special care, and by all means do not give any indication that you are aware of his motivation, or he will lose face and the whole thing will boomerang on you.

If this sounds suspiciously Machiavellian, perhaps we should for a moment examine the way things really are in the world. To most businessmen, the word "manipulation" if used to describe their actions is an affront to their honor, and there is a tendency for them to overreact defensively. But, whether we like to face it or not, the fact is that a large part of managerial action *is* manipulative in nature. The essence of management *is* to predict and control human behavior.

If the manager manipulates others for his personal aggrandizement he is culpable; if he manipulates others for the good of the organization and with no thought of personal gain, he is simply doing what his job description says he should be doing. This is a distinction difficult for some managers to make, but it is nevertheless there.

Another way of putting it would be to state that the entire relationship between you and your vendors is one ongoing series of "give and take" actions that in the long run must balance out very closely. It is unrealistic to expect that either of you should find yourself continually on the plus side of the ledger, or the one who is doing the giving will naturally be going broke. There has to be something in it for both parties, or the entire relationship is unrealistic and incapable of being sustained. Keeping this constantly in mind will help us maintain perspective, and we can continue doing business indefinitely under this sort of balancing act.

RELATIONSHIPS WITH MULTIPLE SOURCES

Most companies, either manufacturing or service, find it necessary to procure goods or services from several sources. If you buy each product from one source only, your relationships with the vendors are of one kind; if several firms are selling you the same product, the interfaces between these vendors present some special problems that must be approached differently.

The former situation is less complex, but there are still several basic considerations in purchasing from more than one source. The first is to ensure that all vendors believe you operate under a uniform purchasing policy—that all vendors are essentially treated alike in the basics. This is often a difficult

93

psychological selling job to accomplish, because of the varying personalities of the representatives involved. As you first meet the people from new sources, you will find there is a wide variety in the speed with which rapport is established between you and them. Furthermore, if an "old" vendor sees a new sales representative quickly become a "member of the club," jealousies may be engendered that will cloud your relations with the earlier contact.

Second, make sure that you communicate to *all* vendors the general nature of your complete purchasing needs. Not only should they know the scope of your procurement activities, but they should also be advised whenever your firm makes a new "make or buy" decision that will affect your future purchasing needs. If they are going to lose some old business because you have decided to manufacture a subassembly yourself, they have a right to know this as soon as possible, so that they can rearrange their manufacturing and sales schedules. If, on the other hand, you have decided to buy a part that you previously manufactured yourselves, vendors of that item will want to become competitive for the new business as soon as possible, and this is only fair.

Third, it is mandatory that your vendors have a clear picture of the business philosophy of your top management. They need to know how your business is run so that they can be of better service to you. This fact can have wide ramifications. For example, if your company executives are largely "Theory Y," they will have some strong beliefs about the kind of labor relations that should exist in their sources of procurement. Or if your top management people are associated with the National Alliance of Businessmen, they will have more than a passing interest in the JOBS program, and in all likelihood will be cooperating in the hiring of the disadvantaged. For this reason, they will almost certainly insist that you make your purchases from a source that is an Equal Employment Opportunity firm.

This is not, of course, a one-way street. The operating principles of your vendors can have various effects on your relationships with them in your enterprise, and you should be aware of these principles so that you can do effective planning in making your purchases.

The second multiple-source situation, wherein you are purchasing the same materials from more than one source, presents much more complex relationships. You will have to live with the fact that there will certainly be constant infighting and guerrilla warfare among the vendors to get a larger share of your business. Up to a point, this can work to your advantage, but it can also lead to open hostilities and actions that can be embarrassing or actually damaging to you.

One tactic you should use is to try to minimize the number of times when two or more vendors visit you simultaneously, with the objective always being zero simultaneous visits. Although it may cause you some extra—even repetitive—work, you should give each vendor the courtesy of your complete attention when discussing his product and your company's needs. He has his personal pride and dignity to consider just as you do.

In the event that a vendor makes an unannounced visit while you are talking with another vendor, keep them isolated from each other. The one who came without the appointment can have no real quarrel with you if he has to wait a reasonable length of time before seeing you, just as you become inured to the prospect of a long wait if you go to your doctor's office without having made an appointment. This policy will help convince the competing vendors that you are treating them all essentially the same. If they feel that all the starting blocks on the track are evenly placed, their attitudes toward you will be much more conducive to overall pleasant contacts.

There is one advantage to having multiple sources for the same product that you can exploit to the hilt without endangering your relationships, because it is completely objective in nature. Namely, you have a built-in quality control that will require little personal policing on your part. If one company's shipments consistently contain more rejects than another company's, simply presenting this statistic should be sufficient to get the problem cleared up. The alternative is starkly obvious to the offender.

To recapitulate, this chapter has been concerned with the nature of your relationships with your suppliers (of either products or services). The basic difference from the situation discussed in the preceding chapter is that you have much greater control as the customer than when you are the vendor. One of the critical aspects of your relationships with vendors is that you must carefully plan the time you allot to their representatives. It is easy for them to attempt to monopolize your working day to a point where the time involved becomes dysfunctional.

Also, you must exercise your sensitivity in identifying those necessary times when you feel you have a right to put the squeeze on a vendor for a special service or an accelerated delivery date. Of course, like anything else, if this is overworked, you are jeopardizing the good will of the vendor.

You must continually monitor the quality control of your

vendors. The fact that they were able to meet your specifications the first time around does not automatically ensure that their quality cannot slip. It's your job to see that this doesn't happen.

If your relationship with a vendor is a good one, there will be times when he will give you gratuitous help you neither expected nor asked for. This is a concrete example of the benefits of maintaining a good working climate with all your vendors. The most complex situations arise when you are dealing with multiple supply sources, and these require some special thought and handling.

CHAPTER VI

COMMUNITY RELATIONSHIPS

OUR CULTURE has become so complex that we must, just to live in it, constantly enlarge the circles of people with whom we interface. In other words, it would not be possible to be a successful manager in American business or industry today without taking into account the impact of the business on the community, and that of the community on the enterprise.

YOUR COMPANY AND THE COMMUNITY

The growth of social consciousness among members of management has been phenomenally fast during the past few years—but it had a long way to go. For generations, the manager showed little if any concern about the relationship of his firm to the community, unless he was thinking of the community in terms of customers only. To have suggested to this man that his firm owed something to society would have elicited raucous laughter or simply a quick dismissal of the idea.

The simple fact remains that a company or a corporation is a citizen of the community just as much as the people who comprise it, because the company is also made up of people. The manager must come to agree that he has a responsibility to see that the company is a good citizen, and must realize that in the future an even greater portion of his work efforts will be in this direction. Management at every level must do its planning and implementation of policy and procedures with full cognizance of the impact they will have on the local area. If there is the slightest indication that a policy could cause harm to the community, it must be discarded, for in the long run what is bad for the locale in which the business is located is bad for the business.

Corporate citizenship in the community carries with it many of the same duties and responsibilities that individual citizenship does. Company management must be concerned with local government, and often with the county, state, and federal governments as well. This is of course particularly true in the area of taxation, which can make or break the business firm. A company's executives may make a considered decision to campaign actively among their people for or against certain local candidates who have taken stands on issues pertinent to carrying on the business. Even should such a situation not arise, the company still has the duty of continually urging its employees to get out and vote. Every year, increasing numbers of firms are giving their employees paid released time in reasonable amounts so that they can vote on election day.

Ecological questions are usually the stickiest problems that business firms face. There are some industries which by their very nature contribute large amounts of pollution to the surrounding air or water. We all know some members of this long list: plants for aluminum reduction, plants that produce paper pulp, steel mills—make your own list. Sometimes total correction of these evils is an impossibility if the industry is to go on; in other cases, removing the pollutants is so prohibitively expensive that the enterprise concerned literally can't afford to do it. Nevertheless, the company unquestionably has a civic duty to continue to work on the problem, and to go as far as it can to alleviate a bad condition.

This matter of business's consideration for the community is not a one-way street. After all, the company does contribute a payroll and products or services that are of great utility to the entire area. An enterprise has every right to expect and receive the same consideration from the community that an individual does. This is true for police protection, fire protection, fair treatment in tax assessments, and all other areas where the business and the community interact in any way.

It is management's responsibility to communicate this concept of company citizenship within the community, which is still new to many people, to each of its employees. They must be told that their management is aware that we all live together, and that certain reciprocal duties are ongoing and unavoidable. It is essential that all people in the company be convinced of their management's sincerity in this area. Merely paying lip service to the concept will carry no clout with the employees; they must know for certain that the company is serious about being a good citizen.

One unfortunate fact sometimes makes the company's work in this area difficult. This is that in some places any initiation of action by a company in the community is looked upon with suspicion by the general public because they feel the action must be self-serving. The belief that a business firm will be more guilty of such venality than a given private citizen is hard to justify, but the idea is there and can be hard to shake. In this case, management's public relations task is obvious. In some way, they are going to have to get the message to the community that they are *not* purely selfish in their objectives.

There are many examples of totally good relationships between a business and the community, and these have certainly not sprung up overnight. They are the result of just as much careful planning and good engineering as goes into the development of company products. The coordination of a project to better relations with the community rests squarely on the shoulders of company top management, and they will delegate segments of the job to lower levels of management as they see fit. The objective is to get every member of management involved and committed in some way on an ongoing basis. Moreover, it is just as necessary to control and monitor these efforts as it is to control and monitor internal aspects of the business.

Lest a misunderstanding should arise here, let me emphasize that conformity to company policy in matters of public relations must never be allowed to interfere with any employee's individual integrity and right to make personal decisions. Naturally, these days most of us will not stay long in the employ of a company whose philosophy is too far out of line with our own. There is too much managerial mobility for this to be necessary.

THE MANAGER AS A COMPANY REPRESENTATIVE

As was implied above, the manager must arrive at a basic accommodation between his philosophy and that of the company's in order to keep a viable working relationship between the two. Once this has been done, the manager must remember from then on out that his or her personality can never be divorced from that of the company whenever public appearances are made. You *are* the company to the public. It takes legalistic terminology to insure that any statement you make as a private citizen could not involve the company in some way or another. And even if you did use this terminology, a large percentage of the general public would blandly ignore it and make a direct association between what you say or write and the company itself.

During a time of rather hectic student unrest on a university campus, a professor from the university and his wife went together to a small town upstate so that the professor could keep a breakfast speaking engagement the next morning with a group of the town's businessmen. The night before the engagement, the couple was identified as being "from the university" as they were about to go in to dinner at the town restaurant. The two of them finally got a chance to eat at about 10:00 P.M.—after a very harrowing and vigorous defense of the integrity of the university as an institution. That particular faculty member realized keenly thereafter that he was a 24-hour public relations representative of the university.

You are an agent of your employer, *especially as you make public contacts*. This means that not only you but the firm can be held accountable for what you say and do. This can be a terrifying and intimidating realization to a new manager—or an old one, for that matter. It may have a tendency to inhibit some people to the extent that they become practically mute when away from their place of employment, and this, naturally, is just as bad for relations as when one speaks too freely.

There are certain techniques that will help a manager

to avoid this sort of frustration. First, in conversations with people who do not work for your company, get into the habit of anticipating possible booby traps of misunderstanding. Practice empathizing with your listeners, and try to predict how you would react in their position if *you* were listening to what you were saying, or seeing what you were doing. This one little habit alone will prevent 90 percent of possible unfortunate situations. Second, make certain that you close the communication loop. Force feedback from your listeners or observers, to see how they have been interpreting what you said. It is often possible to prevent or correct misunderstandings in their infancy; to rectify them in their adolescence or maturity becomes a Herculean task. Third, invite, with both verbal and nonverbal cues, free expression from the person or persons with whom you are interacting. This will in most cases give you an excellent opportunity to examine their particular biases and convictions, thus permitting you to avoid a dangerous area before you ever get into it.

Another facet to the role of company representative is that the manager must be ready at all times to interpret for the public any policy of his employer's which by the furthest stretch of the imagination has any public impact. In order to do this, it is of course necessary that he understand this policy completely, including its intent and the proposed method of implementation. In other words, he can't ever afford to be guilty of peddling misinformation, or he may complicate an already sticky situation beyond repair. One of the duties of the manager is to insist on having the correct information on any given piece of policy—and to pursue, if necessary, the correct authority within the company until he gets it. It is an easy and human mistake for your management to assume that the intent and implications of an action they are considering are plain to the casual observer. Therefore, they may automatically assume that you, as a member of their management, will fully understand the meaning of what is going on.

There are some special cases worthy of note in discussing the manager's role a company representative. One is the situation where his employer is the biggest employer—perhaps the sole employer—in the community. The managers of such a company must be prepared to be the recipients of a special kind of hostility from everyone in the community who is not employed by the firm. Employees of a giant West Coast airframe company became inured—eventually—to hearing "Oh, so you work at the 'Lazy O'?" The fact of the matter was that the management of that company were accustomed to higher salaries and more responsible positions than the national median for management people. People's resentment of that calumny, natural as it was, made community relations between the company and the rest of the city strained at best. The fact that this enterprise practically supported the entire area was not considered germane by the rest of the population.

The opposite of this situation can also be traumatic for the manager. If you are employed by a comparatively small company, your natural ego involvement and personal pride may force you into a pugnaciously defensive attitude that is abrasive to the general public. They will naturally wonder what you are trying to prove by your apparently hostile attitude toward them.

Finally, a word must be said about the biggest single danger the manager faces in his public relations context: his social life. In the regimen of cocktail parties, golf clubs, bridge games, and small dinner parties so familiar to members of management lie some potential sand traps with regard to community relationships. The manager must never find that "his mouth has started before his mind is engaged." In the euphoria of a pseudo-secure situation of socializing, many a company has suffered nearly irreparable damage to its public image. Your contacts will remember tomorrow in an entirely different light what you said in jest and thought they would interpret harmlessly.

All of this certainly does not mean that you should remain mute or become a robot. It means only that you should be constantly aware of the possible false implications of what you say or do in public. Remember, in communications of any sort, it is not what you say or do that is important, but how it is interpreted by the receiver.

Let's stop for a moment to assess whether we have over-emphasized the negative side of the entire matter. Certainly we should never get "uptight" in our interfaces with the public away from work. The higher our anxiety level is in our contacts with "outsiders," the more likely we are to make some silly error that will cause us trouble. The trick is to strike a balance between alertness and naturalness. Don't try to be anyone but yourself in your contacts with those outside the company, for you will inevitably be found out, and any work you have previously done will be completely vitiated. Every one may love a fat man, but nobody loves a phony. Be yourself, but be a self who has done his or her homework meticulously and with loving care.

In summary, the way you represent your employer to the general public will inevitably depend on the state of your general mental health. Only when you have a feeling of personal security can you present a readable and acceptable picture of your employer to those you meet with outside the company environs. Be sure of your homework, so that you know your statements are true; get feedback; be prepared to defend vigorously the posture your company has adopted; read the signals you get from your contacts on the outside; watch your words in social situations; but, above all, keep yourself in balance, so that your self-confidence and personal security can carry you through any interactions you may have with those predisposed to be less than understanding of your firm's position. Then you will be able to carry with honor the colors of your employer in the environment in which you are located.

DETERMINING KEY CONTACTS

If the manager is to be effective in his role as a company representative in the community, he must be selective in choosing his contacts, in the interests of saving time. In every area, there are some citizens who have much larger spheres of influence than lesser-known residents. Note that it does not automatically follow that a judge, or a prominent doctor, or an elected official, will necessarily exert the greatest amount of influence in the town or city. The late Leander Perez was an absolute dictator behind the scene in Louisiana politics while only a small minority of the citizenry recognized his name. It is the manager's responsibility to use his best efforts to ferret out these significant personages, and concentrate on building rapport and mutual respect with them.

If you are successful in this, you will have a much greater impact on company public relations than if you had tried hit-or-miss excessive expenditures of time and effort. We are here invoking the well-known principle of group dynamics that if you have control over the informal leadership of the group you will not have to spend much time with the rest of the members. They will go your way as the natural followers of the informal leader.

Of course, we should not belittle the possible effects of the power of well-known celebrities. It is never a mistake to discuss thoroughly with these people the ramifications of your company's business philosophy and methods of operation. They would probably never take the trouble to come out publicly of their own volition to champion your enterprise, but it could be immensely to your advantage if they were able to correct misinformation expressed by other individuals or groups.

Learning the necessary finesse in approaching key figures is a fine art, and entails the use of both empathy and intuition on the part of the manager. Implicit here is the fact that you must understand, in depth, the personalities and behavior patterns of each of the key figures. In other words, you will never be able to develop any sort of simplistic or rigid formula that will work in all cases as a method of building good public relations. (As you might already suspect, this individualized study of the various powerful figures you have identified in your community will be a time-consuming exercise.) However, there are a few general principles we might mention.

One principle is that cultivation of contacts should be made in the most natural-seeming context. If you come into contact with one of your target figures through a common membership in the Lions Club or a lodge, make your first tentative overtures in this setting. It is the most natural thing in the world for two people, as their acquaintanceship matures, to spend considerable time discussing their respective businesses or occupations. This occurs because nearly all people feel most comfortable in discussing the two things they think they know best—themselves and their working activities. Well-trained interviewers in every field capitalize on this phenomenon.

Another, and more difficult point, is to steel yourself to the realization that a confrontation will inevitably occur somewhere along the line. You may discover that your two enterprises have opposing basic philosophies or methods of doing business. Or again, perhaps the present activities of your two concerns are in direct opposition to each other for the moment. It is far better to discuss this openly than to try to avoid the subject. You may or may not be able to reconcile your differences in the process of exploring them, but meeting the problem head-on will at least breed respect between you, and can lay the foundation for much more fruitful discussions later, when the scene has changed. Some of the finest and strongest friendships in the world have grown from an original situation of distrust or active opposition between two individuals.

The smart manager will make an effort to cultivate a wide variety of key contacts in the community. The greater the number of companies, products, services, and disciplines represented among your contacts, the greater will be the total effect of your work in public relations. It takes delicate handling, but you should not veer away from the possibility of simultaneously pursuing figures in firms that are in active competition with each other. So long as you keep your references to their competitors fair and accurate, and are certain to show no visible bias in either direction, they can have no basic quarrel with your tactics if they have the least vestige of fair-mindedness.

Then there is the "hairiest" matter of them all: What should be your attitude and posture in the community as you meet representatives of your own competitors? Should an antiseptic distance be maintained between you, with little or no actual contact, or should your instinct tell you to learn all you can about your enemy? Here again, there is no simple answer to this question. Each case must be decided on its own merit, and the answer will be a function of your personality and that of your competitive contact. In one medium-sized city, two heavily competitive medical representatives were both highly successful because they had come to respect each other personally and steadfastly refused to denigrate each other's companies to any of their customers or professional contacts. Their individual professionalism carried them through what could easily have degenerated into a nasty dog-fight without either company or either representative suffering in the slightest. It went so far that after a few years of this kind of relationship they came to an occasional cautious comparing of notes on the idiosyncracies of their doctors and druggists and hospital administrators.

It is obvious that many human factors and other variables are involved in the matrix the manager builds for himself in his community relationships. It requires no mean agility on his part to deal with the constant changes that will occur in this mix. This managerial activity will continue to demand great perceptivity and immediate reaction to perceived change. It is a significant part of the challenge inherent in the job of today's manager.

Building the Company Image Through Your Employees
To a large degree, the sum of managerial effort in the area of public relations will determine the company's community

image. The way in which you yourself represent the firm, and the attitudes of your carefully developed contacts, will help form a picture of your firm that will pervade the site of your enterprise. However, another aspect of community relations must not be overlooked. Managers are not the only employees of your firm who live in the town or city. There are other employees who have many more contacts with the public than management, because there are so many more of them. We are referring, of course, to your hourly employees.

Some hourly employees will be conscious of how they affect the public image of their company, but we can't *assume* this to be true in any individual case. Part of the managerial job is to make a conscious effort to develop in every employee a sense of pride about how his employer is viewed in the community. This can be done only when the employees, as persons, become committed to the enterprise and concerned about their reputation as employees of the company.

Most of us—even managers—have difficulty in committing ourselves to an impersonal entity called simply a "company." Most of us commit ourselves to people, not things. Accordingly, the successful manager will find his people committing themselves to him or her, rather than to an impersonality. Or, to state it another way, you *are* the company to your people. It may add heavily to an already onerous load of managerial responsibility, but you should strive to develop the type of relationship where the people who report directly to you will not consciously do anything that will derogate *your* reputation in the community. Once personal loyalty has been engendered, it is much easier for you logically to expand this concept to include all other facets of the company.

We are working here with the personal motivations of individuals, and those motivations will be as varied as the people themselves. Essentially, we are back full circle to a basic we can never lose sight of: There can be no managerial progress in working with employees' motivation until the supervisor/manager knows two things—himself, and the people *as individuals*. This concept is certainly not new, but it is hardly possible to emphasize it too heavily. One young manager made a fine name for himself in his firm because his people identified so closely and loyally with him and his organization. When questioned, he made no secret of his methods. He told anyone asking him that he made careful plans to "casually," or "accidentally," have several five-minute conversations per month, *on nonbusiness matters*, with each employee. Although the conversations were on the surface totally nondirective, in actuality his intent was to discover as much as he could about every employee, up to just this side of the invasion of privacy. Of course, in their presence he took no notes except mental ones, but he did keep a coded file on every one of his employees safely under lock and key in his office.

Some of the direct results of this managerial technique were immediately apparent. First, team spirit became superb in the manager's own crew. Second, his employees would—and many times did—respond far beyond the ordinary call of duty when the pressure was on their boss. Third, his department's performance became a model for the entire plant. Fourth, and most important for our discussion here, this pride of membership in what they considered to be an elite group carried over to the employees' nonworking hours, and they became extraordinarily fine company ambassadors in all of their community relations. Perhaps the most amazing thing about the entire matter was that the supervisor was not notably extroverted. Sincere and honest, yes, but not an exceptionally outgoing and charismatic leader. He simply converted a managerial technique to his own and the company's advantage. Needless to say, his own upward mobility suffered no visible harm from this kind of performance.

How Much Community Service?

There can be no question that managerial public service in the community has positive effects on the image of the company represented. This much is a "given" in the minds of most managers. The question remaining to be solved individually by each manager is "How much, and where?"

The "how much" question is chiefly a personal one, of course. But sometimes the company must be brought in on the matter. If a manager goes overboard, or appears to, in the amount of time he donates to the public in any kind of service, his peers and his supervisors are likely to start questioning whether he is doing his basic job at work. Some managers become quite paranoid about this, and shudder if they are "volunteered" by their company as a loaned executive for the local Community Chest drive, thinking that perhaps they are being made available because they were judged to be producing the least for their company, and are therefore expendable. The best approach, of course, is for each manager to counsel with his superiors and negotiate with them the "proper" amount of time, either personal or that of the firm, to be expended on public service.

Once this has been established, a second major decision has to be made: where to offer one's services. Should you go to the area which, of all the areas needing help, interests you the most? Or should you enter the field where the need is greatest, period? One could make a convincing argument that the manager will be most effective in areas where his interest lies, since he will start any work he does already well-motivated. On the other hand, if he enters a neglected but needy area, he may experience even more personal satisfaction, and anything he accomplishes there will show up well when the kudos are handed out, both for the manager and his firm. This is one of the times when pure drudgery may well prove rewarding in the extreme.

Before committing yourself, you should also give earnest thought to the reconciliation of the two schedules involved—your own working cycle, and the periodicity of demand that arises in many kinds of volunteer labor. Are there likely to be clashes between the two that could prove disastrous to both efforts? You should be sure this will not happen before offering your services to any volunteer effort.

There is a possibility that entering community service will have some serendipitous effects on your job performance. Work it is, yes, but perhaps just the change of pace from what you do at the office or in the plant will be refreshing and will revitalize your attitude toward your regular job. Moreover, it has happened more than once that something learned on a volunteer job was directly transferable to the job situation, with beneficial results there. This is known as the "double dip" in community service.

One caution must always be observed. *Never* accept a community obligation unless you are 99 percent certain you can carry it through gracefully and successfully. The boomerang effect of a missed community assignment can be murderous to both your own public relations and those of your company. Much better not to start it at all than to botch it up to everyone's ultimate disadvantage.

Another facet of responding to community calls is well known, but still bears repeating: Those who do, get asked again. One executive in a Southern plant of a large aluminum company responded favorably to an innocuous-looking request from the local Camp Fire Girls Executive to act as training director for the council for "a year." It seems she felt that there were some training manuals which should be rewritten, and discerned some areas where new ones should be created. The man did the job with dispatch and distinction, and was properly thanked for his service. To his bewildered amazement, he somehow found himself elected as the president of the council for the next year, and was virtually blackmailed into serving a second year as president. This job he found demanding beyond belief; there were times when it seemed as if a question existed as to which was his principal job— managing at the plant, or serving the Camp Fire Girls. The obvious moral is that those who have been willing volunteers in the past are quite likely to be imposed on unless they know how to say "No!" convincingly at the right time. And, logically enough, a man who develops a silhouette of good service in one community agency can expect to receive frequent requests from other areas of need. The final response to the question "How much community service?" is answerable only by the manager himself, and will depend greatly on his stamina.

To sum it up, community relationships are obviously of great importance to the overall success of your enterprise.

The individual manager is regarded as a representative of his company when he is interfacing with those outside the company in the community, and people's opinions of him can have a visible effect on the firm's total achievements. His own personality is sometimes submerged in the role of a company agent.

Every member of management must give considerable thought and care to the picking of key contacts in the community. Some people can be of immense value to your firm because of their personal influence and charisma in the town. It is much more important to have rapport with a few of these people than with dozens or even hundreds of people of less importance in the community.

Every contact a manager makes in the community should be done with the definite thought in mind of helping his employer's public image. You don't have enough total energy available to risk spinning your wheels in ineffective or damaging public contacts. This point is closely tied to the question of how much community service should be undertaken by a manager, and the latter is a personal decision that each individual must make for himself.

CHAPTER VII

DATA FLOW—OUTGOING

COMMUNICATIONS are the nerve center as well as the muscular tonus of all interpersonal relationships. In management, the telling/listening interface comprises more than 90 percent of business communications, while all other forms of communication make up the other 10 percent. In this chapter, we are going to be concerned with what *we* transmit—what we tell others.

WHAT TO TELL YOUR BOSSES

In examining the managerial communicative process, you are of course vitally concerned with what you tell those above you in the hierarchy, because it has such a visible effect on their evaluation of you as a manager. In this area, there are some broadly generalized truisms that it will be to your advantage to remember.

First: Tell your boss what he wants to hear, *when you can*. There is nothing intrinsically servile or self-seeking in being the bearer of good news, and you should take advantage of this fact whenever you can. It is perfectly understandable psychologically that the "good news" man takes on a new aura, at least for the moment. Make every effort to be the first one there with the delicious tidbit you know your bosses are going to thank you for. Even the second person there gathers some brownie points, but nothing like the number credited to the first bearer of the news. It goes without saying that you had better be certain of the authenticity of your item, because there can be a devastating backlash when bosses find out that some pleasant news was just a mirage.

Second: Tell your boss what he *doesn't* want to hear when you know it is necessary to his safety and the performance of your group. If he gets petulant or a bit irked with you at first, it will pass, and his reasoning will eventually win out over his emotions, with no permanent damage to your relationships with those upstairs. In fact, the final outcome may be a deepened respect for you, for bosses, as practicing managers, know how much courage it takes to tell a superior that a serious hitch has developed somewhere in the works. The same necessity for speed applies here as in the preceding situation. Try to be the first one to get the news to those affected, because the more quickly a sore spot in the body politic is discovered, usually the less depressing and severe will be the remedy for the trouble. It always helps in this situation if you have been able to gather enough data to suggest a possible way to rectify the error (of commission or omission) that has resulted in a trouble spot. This might sound like the diagnostician leading his patient directly to the waiting surgeon, but the sooner necessary drastic action is taken, the sooner will be the recovery—and, in all probability, the more complete.

Third: Don't bother your superiors with the trivia of

your operations—unless you have the misfortune to work for a perfectionist, in which case load him down with every tiny detail you can scrounge up from your area. Those higher than you in the organization chart have a right to be treated with respect, and part of your job is to be a screening device for what is passed upstairs. Your company's communication network could not function if managers did not exercise selectivity in imparting material in any direction, and you should keep this in mind at all times. However, if you have reason to believe that a seemingly minor detail will be of value to your managers in completing their overview of the "big picture," don't hesitate to pass it on, with a mention of your reason for doing so. The jewels in a watch are tiny, but they run the whole works.

Fourth: Apply a simple criterion to whatever you transmit up the line. Ask yourself whether you, if you were in your boss's place, would want to know the information in question. If the answer is a qualified "yes," send it on. Of the two sins, overcommunication is much less grave than undercommunication. Your boss may become impatient if he hears the same thing too many times, but he will be completely paranoid if he suspects that vital information is being withheld from him. The little ploy of prefacing your transmittal with "Did you know that—?" will many times turn away wrath. There are also other factors to be considered in deciding what you will send upward. The field of management is rapidly being complicated with new methods, new tools, new types of organizational structures, and the new and different breeds of employers with whom you will be dealing.

The fifth precept, which applies to all other areas of communication as well, is to cultivate a sense of timing. Unfortunately, there is always a wrong time for telling the right information. Be sensitive to the situation your supervisors are finding themselves in at any given moment. If it's budget time for the division, the general manager of your department will not be very attentive to minor operational details. If an order for one of your prime customers is in difficulty, think several times before derailing your boss's train of thought to consider a matter of lesser importance. If upper management is deeply absorbed in the formulation of an important new piece of policy, make your own decision and tell them about it afterwards. The only thing at stake here is your job, but that is on the line either way you go. Welcome to the club!

To recapitulate: What you tell your superiors must be both utilitarian and timely. The communications you send your bosses are the warp and woof of your relationships with them, and the twin goals of quality and quantity apply here just as they do to the production of your company's products or services. The manager must get his work done chiefly through others, so his efficiency will ultimately be measured largely by his effectiveness as a communicator.

What to Tell Your People

Your responsibility in communicating down the line to your people is in some respects similar to your responsibility in communicating up, but there are some subtle differences. The ancient managerial disease of refusing to divulge information necessary to subordinates has not disappeared from the American business scene; we all like to know something that others do not. In many cases, the guilty manager is not deterred by the knowledge that this lack of information will adversely affect the work of his people. The one inviolable tenet should be that if the information is important to the operation of the group there can be no excuse for withholding it.

If we can actually establish a degree of difference between the two situations, then it is this: It is more important that subordinates be told bad news than that it be passed upstairs. This has as much to do with group morale as anything else. Our people are not dummies—they can perceive the usual clues that indicate trouble somewhere in the organization. Unless they are promptly told the truth, they will be fecund in dreaming up worse situations than the one that actually exists. The tragic result here is that the manager may find his best people sharpening up their résumés and beginning to look around. Many good organizations have been made deathly ill—or have died—because bits of bad news have been withheld from the people concerned. We all want to see our enemy's face; fighting in the dark is the scariest trouble one can find himself in.

On the happier side, you should never pass up an opportunity to communicate good news. Most important, you should never let especially good performance of either individuals or groups go unrecognized. Lack of expected recognition ranks high on the list of employee dissatisfiers. It is a hopeful sign that awareness of the value of nonmaterialistic motivators is spreading rapidly through the ranks of management. But the one area standing to benefit most from this idea still has to be penetrated: labor/management relations. We are still lumbering along under an antiquated and dysfunctional system of grievance settlement that gives little recognition to the fact that an employee can—and often does—hurt elsewhere than in his pocketbook. An adjustment to this fact of life could help to significantly retard the spiraling rate of inflation in our country.

More specifically, there are some generic kinds of information that every manager must be prepared to give to his people automatically. First on the list is new or changing technical information about the processes and jobs in which they are involved. *Give them this information long enough in advance of its implementation to allow an employee to adjust.* In most cases it's not the change itself that is upsetting to people, but rather the suddenness of its imposition. They need a chance to revise their thinking.

Second: Pass on any ancillary information that is connected but perhaps not necessarily critical to proposed changes or modifications. The more we know about something new, the easier it becomes to make a transition into a new scene.

Third: The manager should be most meticulous about briefing his people concerning new company policy or procedures not directly connected with their work situation. The more we know about the company or agency we work for (if it is a decent one), the easier it is to identify with it and feel a part of the group. Management has traditionally fallen into a trap here. In most enterprises, the company has a much more complicated hierarchy, and consists of many more echelons, than do its employees' unions. In transmitting information about a proposed new policy to a union, policy makers forget that this information will reach the grass roots of the union much faster than it will reach their management. First-line supervisors and managers are understandably infuriated when they hear rumors from their own people about new proposals (later proved to be true) that they had known nothing about from their own management.

Fourth: An alert manager will go further in his communication with his people than just passing along information concerning his own enterprise. Most employees have a perfectly predictable selfish interest in knowing how the competition is doing. Their job security may be at stake, so they have a right to know how their company is doing as compared to the rest of the field. In fact, as a manager you could do much worse than to share with your people information concerning the economy as a whole. They may or may not show any visible signs of interest in this sort of data, but at least it will be evidence to them that you are concerned with your employees as individual human beings, rather than as adjuncts to the machinery. Moreover, you will be approaching them on an intellectual level equal to your own, and this is important.

Fifth: Be careful to keep your people up to date on the state of the art in your function or discipline, whether or not new developments will have any direct impact on your operation. If there is any sort of identification present, the employee will want to know how his company stands technically in comparison to the rest of the industry.

Sixth: Share immediately with your subordinates whatever pertinent information comes your way about other departments or functions in the company. We all have a natural curiosity about our neighbors; your people will thank you for making them more knowledgeable about people elsewhere in the organization.

In your communications with your people, once more an empathic approach will stand you in good stead. If you were in their shoes, would you want, or need, to have in your possession the facts you know? If the answer is "yes," you know what to do about it.

The manner of communicating is important, and should be the result of some careful planning on your part. Some situations practically beg for a little showmanship in communicating them; others are best played straight, with no emotionalism or hoopla attached. Don't forget, too, that your timing in passing along information is just as important with your people as it is when you are communicating up the line. The same sorts of variables are operant here, but you are in a better position to make a reasoned decision about when to spread the word. Good downward communication can do more than almost any other single factor in determining your reputation with your people as a manager.

WHAT TO TELL YOUR PEERS

There is a special kind of ambivalence associated with your communication with your peers. You need them and their cooperation badly to do your own work effectively, just as they need you. Yet you are in direct competition with them on the road to further promotions, and all of you are aware of this. You feel constrained whenever you are talking with them, and you weigh and evaluate each piece of information before you share it with any manager on your level, either in your own or other departments. This schizoid state will persist and grow as you climb higher on the managerial ladder.

In spite of this, there are certain things you *must* talk about freely with other managers at your level. First, there is an irreducible minimum of information that must be shared between departments in their coordinative efforts. Your peers need to know where you stand on the road to your common objectives at any given time; similarly, you can't operate effectively unless you know where *they* are. The more promptly and completely these data are passed back and forth, the cleaner and smoother will be the enterprise's total effort.

Second, it will often be to your advantage to tell your peers things you have discovered that are germane to their area that you have reason to believe they don't know. Your peers' subordinates will tell you things that they would never take directly to their bosses. The same thing, of course, will happen to you, and you will certainly be grateful to learn important facts about your group from whatever source possible. The best source for this kind of information is usually the men and women on the production floor, or the nonmanagerial employees in the office areas. These are the people who really know what is going on—or what is not going on that should be. This points up the importance of your cultivating rapport with people in all areas and at all levels.

Third, don't hesitate to talk with your peers about what you consider might be an improvement in their operation. Many times the uninvolved bystander has a clearer view of the overall picture than the person with direct responsibility for its operation. By the same token, you should not be too proud to listen to suggestions from your peers about your work. Credit can be freely given to the originator of an idea, because it is your work that will benefit from a good one, and, after all, your managers are more interested in results than in how the results were obtained.

Fourth, communicate freely and candidly with your peers when they have had an obvious success on a project. I have already mentioned the importance of giving your people recognition for a good performance; your peers desire recognition just as much as you and your people do.

Fifth, when a gross error has been perpetrated, you should be alert for any kind of cue from the manager involved indicating that he would not be averse to discussing it with you.

This situation, the opposite of the preceding one, presents one of the more delicate areas of peer communications. But if the manager in question is at all objective in evaluating his or her performance, there can often be great value in a common analysis of what went wrong and why. Not *who* was wrong, but *what*. If it develops naturally, this kind of a session will often put you in the role of the nondirective counselor: You give a sympathetic and uncritical ear to your peer as he does his own introspective analysis of the problem. This "tuning fork" or "sounding board" role often helps the person in trouble to see things in better perspective. The one thing to remember is that unless your relationship with this peer is especially close, you can seldom afford to initiate the activity. The peer must come to you with an indication of wanting help before you can get on track toward a solution of the problem.

Good peer communications can significantly improve the overall climate of your total organization. When relationships are easy, and there is trust and confidence along the lateral lines in the organization, things can be made to happen much more easily than when an aura of secretiveness pervades interdepartmental relationships. Keeping things to yourself that are of value to your peers does not usually result in an advantage to you, because they will doubtless be doing the same thing. You need to know the things concerning you; they can benefit from the bits of data you have.

The cultivation of good peer communications is an ongoing effort. You don't make one hard try and then just coast. You should keep on the lookout for significant data to be transmitted across the lines. In other words, the entries in the personal notebook every good manager keeps should not be limited to things that concern him alone. Jot down pertinent items for discussion at an appropriate time later. The fact that you write these items down will reinforce their importance and will help remind you to share them with the proper persons.

The need for effective peer communication increases geometrically with the size of the organization. In a small, tight group the need is self-evident, but as the number of managers increases, there may be a tendency to fractionalize the enterprise into splinter groups of managers who see themselves as self-sufficient. Nothing could be further from the truth than this assumption. The more complex the structure, the easier it is for breaks to occur in the communication chains, with concomitant damage to the whole.

Naturally, a concern with peer communications places an extra burden on your work day, but its importance is such that you can't ignore it or shrug it off as nice but not necessary. Keep the channels open, or you might find them clogged when you really need to use them.

What to Tell the Public

Many of the facets of the manager's role as a community representative of the enterprise were discussed in Chapter VI, but it cannot be amiss to reinforce how important your communications to the "outside world" are to your company and you.

First and foremost: When outside the confines of your company, be sure that no proprietary information is ever inadvertently leaked. We get so used to talking "in house" about these things that we could easily slip and forget our entailed duty of secrecy where new products, new methods, or industry breakthroughs are concerned. If there is the slightest doubt in your mind as to the propriety of mentioning them, forget it.

Second: Accentuate the positive. Take every opportunity to "sell" the contributions your company or agency makes to the public at large. The key to this situation is your manner of communicating. Many take offense if they feel someone is putting a "hard sell" into a conversation or speech made outside the work climate, so choose your wording carefully and be thoroughly perceptive of the cues from your audience as you are talking.

Third: Take extra precautions when talking to the press or to radio or TV people, even if they assure you that you are "off the record." A quote that they attribute to "a high company spokesman" can many times be traced directly to your doorstep simply from the matter that was discussed. Members of the mass media consider that anything they learn is fair game for publication or airing, under the concept of freedom of the press. This puts some special constraints on your ability to talk freely before them. Many companies simply enforce an ironclad rule that no one but the public relations people *ever* talk to news representatives. Of course, if you are the manager principally concerned with a big event in your business that has public import, you will probably be interviewed, but it should be under the firm control and proper guidance of your company PR experts.

Fourth: Seize every opportunity afforded you to congratulate other companies or the community at large for good things that are happening in your area of influence. Special civic accomplishments do deserve recognition, and your awareness of them (ergo your company's awareness of them) should be communicated quickly and thoroughly to the general public. Also, so long as you stick to the strict truth, there can be no harm in recapitulating the contributions that your own business has made.

Fifth: By the same token, when a community problem has been identified, your company, and yourself as one of its managers, can hardly be criticized for making a contribution to the overall discussion. Of course, the reputation of both you and your superiors is put on the line whenever you take a stand on a public issue, but you owe it to yourself and the public at large to stand up and be counted when a controversial issue is being discussed by the community.

Sixth: As a professional manager, you have another audience to whom you should be communicating freely—your industry or profession at large. Whenever you get a chance to be a speaker or discussion leader at a conference attended by your business associates, grab it and run. Just be sure you are running in the right direction, and that you've done some carefully documented homework before you get up before the group. A parallel road is to write articles for your industry or professional journals. In fact, one of the best stimulators to professional growth in management is to discipline yourself to do some writing on a continuing basis. For one thing, the research required will help you to stay on top of progress in your field; for another, the writing itself will help you to formulate a personal perspective on new developments.

All of which brings us once more to the point that continued professional growth in all areas of management is becoming increasingly important to your career. Never again will it be possible for a manager to learn a few generalized methods and continue to use them indefinitely into the future.

The only thing that today's manager can be sure of is that tomorrow's methods will be new, better—and probably more sophisticated. To be competitive, any member of management will find it necessary to continually learn more about his or her field, and this applies to the theory and practice of management itself as well as to technical knowledge in the discipline involved. Our business competition is now, and will continue to be, worldwide. The one fatal sin a manager can commit is to fall into complacency, even for so long as a single breath. The key is to develop mental discipline and to become accustomed to an unceasing learning situation. On the positive side, this is a climate in which the excitement never stops, and you can be sure of one thing: You will never die of boredom if you follow this regimen.

Parenthetically, it is interesting to note the widening interest in the general field of adult education. Industrial psychologists and behavioral scientists in general are undertaking innumerable studies in this area, some dealing with basic theory and some with practical applications. One solid thing we have going for us here is the fact that adult learners are for the most part strongly self-motivated, which means they are already pointed down the road toward a successful learning experience.

So, to come back from this fascinating bypath, today's manager *must* communicate with the public—in self-protection if for no other reason—but it must be done carefully, and with preplanning.

WHAT NOT TO TELL AT ALL

One of the more difficult areas of managerial communications is to make the decision to say or transmit nothing. There are, of course, dozens of reasons that might influence you to remain silent, but there are a few basic ones that deserve some special attention.

First, it is rare indeed when the manager will knowingly pass on a rumor, *even if the rumor is a favorable one.* When a less-than-certain bit of information has bad connotations, it is a near certainty that someone will be hurt by disseminating it. If the rumor is good news and then proves to be false, the backlash from this situation makes the managers who have been instrumental in sending along the false information appear in an exceptionally bad light, to both their peers and the people who work for them. It is a perfectly human characteristic to be alert to what is passing through the rumor mill—sometimes you *do* learn things in advance, and thereby get a chance to prepare for new contingencies. But, over the long haul, it is better not to become involved.

Second, the smart manager will refrain from transmitting anything derogatory to another person unless there is a compelling reason for the good of the business that others know about it. Having the reputation among your fellow managers and your employees of being a person who doesn't have anything bad to say about others is one of the highest accolades that can be accorded to any manager. This is not to imply for a moment that you become namby-pamby or soft. You will simply be cultivating an attitude of not doing harm to your fellow beings, and this is a sign of strength of character rather than weakness.

Third—and this is an obvious one—your lips are sealed when those above you in the hierarchy give you information that they have marked "secret." It may be true—and quite often *is* true—that the reasons for this directive are not valid;

but that is not your decision to make. This is not to say you can't try to influence your superiors to release needed information, but if they refuse, you can do nothing about it until they change their minds.

Fourth, you as a manager should refuse to communicate information to another person when his motive for wanting it is obviously self-service or personal aggrandizement. Your concern is always for the enterprise at large, and something that is done to favor one individual at the expense of the whole concern can never have a beneficent outcome.

You should be constantly on the alert for the above situations. They ordinarily arise suddenly, and you will have only a short time in which to make your decision about whether to communicate. Two things will help you here. The first is the growing bank of dependable data you have accumulated in your experience as a manager. The second is pure intuition—which you will still have to depend on many times, as your interrogator will often count on surprise to force a quick answer from you before you have had a chance to check the facts. Your best protection here is an inner core of sharp alertness beneath a facade of bland cheerfulness.

This chapter has surveyed your personal managerial responsibilities in the communications you transmit. You have a sort of censor's role in what you tell your bosses: You must sort out what they need to know from what could clutter up their operations with needless detail.

So far as your people are concerned, remember the human tendency to want to be the owner of secrets. The criterion: Is this secret *really* necessary? You must see to it that your subordinates have all the information they need to function properly, plus background information that will help them to have a better understanding of the entire scene.

The special problems of communicating with your peers are fairly clear. They must know the things common to your coordinated operations, yet you would be foolish to give them information that could lead to their having an unfair advantage over you in your competition for further advancement.

Your public utterances are of critical importance, both to you and your employers. The best rule of thumb here is ordinarily to leave public statements to those who are specialists in the field. Lastly, there are a number of things that are better never communicated at all. These you will hopefully recognize as they come up, and the decision must be yours.

CHAPTER VIII

DATA FLOW—INCOMING

To CLOSE THE LOOP in communications, it is obviously necessary that we have something coming in as well as going out. But there are some added steps in the receiving of information: The receiver has to translate what he gets, and get some feedback to be sure that he understood what was sent.

OPENING THE DAM UP THE LINE

As the receiver, you are no longer in control of what is being sent. When you are doing the sending, you can choose the content, receiver, and timing, but this is not true when you are the recipient. One of the more difficult situations you can find yourself in is to have above you a line of management that is reluctant to part with information which you need in order to do your job. As noted before, this is unfortunately a fairly common situation. If you are faced with a communications void from above, for whatever reason, there are some ploys you will have to use to break this impasse.

First: If you find yourself in this situation, study it intensively and with the greatest amount of objectivity you can muster. There has to be a reason. Is it perhaps something *you* are doing, or not doing? Are you the only manager who finds himself in trouble because he is not being talked to by those above him in the line? Check with your peers to see whether they've had comparable difficulties, and if you find yourself an unfavored single, then zero in on the possible causes. Do your managers have some real or fancied reason for not giving you their complete trust and confidence? Have you been guilty of real or apparent breaches of security in the past? If so, talk it out with your managers above you. Indicate that you are sensitive to their reactions, and are making a solid effort to repair the damage done a long time ago. They would be less than human if they were to completely refuse to listen to you, and this at least gets the matter out on the table for mutual consideration of methods of repair.

Second: If you are convinced that you are not at fault, the easiest and most obvious thing to do is to ask your management for what you need to know. Be specific. It is entirely possible that they think you already have access to the data you need, and are innocent of any malice in keeping it from you. If this is the case, your troubles are over almost before they have begun. On the other hand, if there is a definite and deliberate blockage from above you, you will have to turn to other ruses to get what you need.

Third: Carry on an active campaign of propaganda for opening the channels. Be a gadfly in the side of top management. It may irritate them, but they can hardly combat you openly without exposing themselves as bad managers of the first order. You have all the logic on your side, and they know it. In other words, implicit in your job description is the duty to train your bosses in their shortcomings whenever they surface. It should not be necessary to say that this requires delicate handling.

Fourth: Go to other sources who have the data you need. In almost every business concern, a large part of all operational information is shared laterally among several departments. Should you find yourself consistently blocked by the line immediately above you, cultivate other sources in other departments where you can bootleg the facts you need. Needless to say, this is indicative of a less than desirable relationship with your superiors, but we live in a real world, and we all do what is necessary to preserve ourselves and get the job done.

Fifth: If it is only your immediate boss who is blocking you, seek a means of bypassing him or her, and make productive contact with the echelon above. This is admittedly a dangerous gambit, but it may be necessary for your survival and continued successful operation. *You must get your needed data.*

Sixth: If it seems necessary, organize your peers and subordinates into a concentrated effort to change top management's policies and attitudes. When downward communications are stagnated simply because it has always been that way, you should organize your forces and attack the problem just as you would any other you face in your business life. List your alternatives, figure the odds, and set your campaign in motion. We must constantly keep in mind the isolation of top management—part of it inherent in the position, and part of it established deliberately to conserve time and minimize interruptions. One of the fallouts of this isolation can be (and often is) a failure to realize what the people below the executive level are thinking, or what they are in need of. To reiterate, the gradual drift toward a drying up of downward communication may not be malicious, but simply a failure to empathize with the lower echelons.

All of the preceding has had a negative cast; while reading it you might have gotten the feeling that you, the manager, are on an advanced patrol in enemy territory during wartime. This is not the intent of this discussion. Communication is largely a frame of mind; the techniques used are of less importance than the intentions of the parties concerned. Unless there is some "meeting of the minds," all the words, writing, and nonverbal cues in the world will be meaningless and not understood. You must *want* to receive just as your superiors must *want* to transmit. Until this commonality of intent has been arrived at, any efforts at communication between levels will be sterile. It will take a little work, by both parties, to achieve an easy understanding.

Siphoning Your Data from Below

The title of this section is not too far-fetched an analogy: The trick in obtaining information from your subordinates is to get the flow started in the first place. In every organization an inertia exists that must be overcome before a natural, ongoing flow of data will be established. In managing incoming communications, your job is to see to it that you do not throw up the same blocks that were mentioned in the preceding section, where we were talking about difficulties in getting information from your superiors.

If you feel you are not getting good communications from below, your first step should be an introspective examination to make certain that *you* are not inhibiting those who report to you, by either your mannerisms, your talk, or departmental procedures. For example, in one large company (which shall be nameless) there was a strict policy which stated that no member of management below the third level could have free access to the books of procedures. How ridiculous can a management get? Are first- and second-line supervisors members of management or not? Not there they weren't!

Next, if this examination does turn up some suspicious items, root them out, lock, stock, and barrel, and replace them with a methodology that will not be dysfunctional. This will entail a complete reorientation of the thinking of your subordinates, since they will have been well conditioned to operate in the old ways. You are going to have to both tell them and *show* them that you have changed your spots, and do want free two-way communications within your department. You probably won't convince them the first time around—and maybe not even the second, third, or fourth. Be patient, and watch for the first signs that they believe things have really changed.

You should remember that their reticence arises out of the same reasons that make *you* averse to talking freely with those above you. They may think that reporting on a bad situation will put them in an unfavorable light with you, the boss. Or they might wrongly assume that they would be considered "informers," with all the opprobrium inherent in that term, and might therefore fail to communicate something important. There are many reasons for reluctance to talk with the boss, and it is your job to ferret them out and destroy them, one by one. Your objective is clear: a smoothly functioning informational chain within your organization that will do its part to get the job done, and nobody can do his best work in the dark.

One useful technique is to set up easily visible incentives for good communications from below. Give recognition—public recognition, that is—when someone has done a good job in giving you the data you need. Make it a significant factor in your merit review system, and let this be known. Everyone responds well to positive reinforcement of his behavior.

Once more, we must mention the matter of building trust and confidence between the two levels. There are many facets to this task, but you will go a long way toward accomplishing it if you make sure that it is easy and simple to get a flow of meaningful communication going both ways through the line.

At this point, it would be useful to define these "good communications" that we have been striving after. First, to be good, a communication must be truthful. One piece of misinformation sent in either direction can wreck a structure it has taken years to build. This is unfortunately true whether the falsehood was intentional or not. The people who were misled will thereafter be doubtful of the veracity of *any* statement sent their way by the offending party.

Second, a good communication must be *replicable*. Another person approaching the data from another direction, and even for a different reason, must arrive at the same answers.

Third, the basic core of meaning in the communication must be conveyed in terms that are understandable to all concerned. This is why the jargons that are the pride and joy of so many specialties and functions are actually dangerous to the health of an organization. There is simply no justification for the perpetuation of use of jargon to bolster the ego of the perpetuators. No person is a true professional unless he can translate his specialty's terminology into a form that can be understood by someone unsophisticated in the area. This is one of the most widespread diseases of our proliferating technology, and must be fought to a finish whenever it is discovered.

Every manager is a communications specialist as an integral part of his or her job. Communications difficulties arise in every managerial job, simply because there are so many aspects of communications that can cause trouble. And what may be supremely simple to transmit in one function may be terrifyingly difficult in another.

Everyone seems to make the basically fallacious assumption that naming a person "manager" means he will automatically be an expert in communication and coordination. One has to *learn* to communicate, just as babies have to learn to walk. Fortunately for all of us, in the past few years there have been significant advances in our understanding of the fundamentals of good communication, and the dissemination of this new knowledge is increasing in a gratifying manner. Nevertheless, it is the responsibility of the individual manager to get his own education in this art, and then to practice it assiduously every minute of every day he is on the job. This last statement is meant in the most literal sense of the words. *At no time* during the business day can the manager forget his duties to be a good communicator, as both a transmitter and a receiver, and to check the feedback in both directions.

What to Expect from Your Peers

The one thing you will definitely never get from your peers in communication is more than you are willing to transmit. They will never knowingly give you an advantage in the competitive managerial scene, any more than you would them. Quid pro quo is the phrase of the day—every day.

The categorical imperative which, of course, you have a right to demand from them is enough data to coordinate your activities with theirs whenever necessary. Willful withholding of this kind of information is a capital crime for a manager, and everyone knows it. It is always wise to carefully screen transmittals from known enemies or recognized shady characters, using whatever devices you find viable for checking on their accuracy and completeness. One of the best ways to accomplish this is to recheck the information through other sources, and these are usually available if you look carefully. In many cases it will not be necessary to take this negative approach toward your peers, but you should be alert for situations where it is warranted.

What you should really be trying to cultivate is the kind of relationship with each of your peers that will result in all of you being willing and able to go beyond what is merely necessary and give one another background information as well. The latter can be especially enlightening and can greatly broaden your perspective. The result of this collective action will be a synergism which will affect your entire organization positively and which can greatly enhance your competitiveness in the industrial or business community.

This entire area of creative group communication approaches, but never quite gets to, the point of a brainstorming session. You have neither the time nor the inclination to engage in extensive subjective discussions with your peers. Rather, ask yourself: How does this particular bit of information affect your scene? What's in it for you? Does it shed new light on what had been a mystery before? You should always apply these criteria in deciding whether incoming data are worth your close consideration. You can be sure your peers will be doing the same to the data they receive from you, and for the same perfectly valid reasons.

For each of your peers, you will have to make an individual judgment about how far beyond the purely business relationship you should go in order to elicit further useful information. This brings us back once again to the point that your interpersonal relationships with peers, just as with those who report to you, will depend on how much you know about them as unique individuals plus how much you know about yourself, and what you can thereby predict from your understanding of these two variables. These same fundamentals apply in our group relationships as managers, a subject that will be examined in a later chapter.

One important phase of communicating with peers is the necessity to develop an excellent feel for the organizational climate throughout the entire enterprise. Styles in business communication among peers will run the entire gamut as you go from company to company. What is de rigueur in one firm, by written or unwritten policy, might be pure poison in its next-door neighbor. You must be sensitive to this kind of thing if you hope to be successful in getting your peers to talk freely with you.

There is one purely logical point that it would be quite naive to overlook: Never expect a peer to communicate anything to you that his boss would be unwilling to tell your boss. At least, he surely wouldn't do it knowingly. This would be pure treachery in anybody's book, and you yourself certainly wouldn't undercut your boss to a member of another department or function. The fact that overcaution in this direction may act as a brake on the communicative process between peers is regrettable, but certainly better than the opposite alternative—a breakdown of trust.

In its more interesting moments, communication with peers becomes a fine art, and one of the more fascinating forms of mental chess. The objective is to stay two or three jumps ahead at all times, and to be planning countermoves for any ploys your peers may come up with. It becomes a major part of the challenge of the field of management.

In this and the preceding chapters, no real emphasis has been placed on the listening side of communication. All of us from time to time fall victim to the disease of selective perception: We see and hear only those things that we are vitally interested in at the moment, and everything we see and hear is colored by our biases and prejudices. The best way to achieve personal objectivity in the managerial world is to practice listening carefully to what others are sending us. *Hear it all, then make your judgments.* An item or so taken out of context can totally change the image received, and you can go away with an "understanding" that would horrify your peer if he knew what was in your mind. Listening properly is a habit that can be achieved only with long practice and limitless patience. Basically, it boils down to a matter of pure courtesy. We expect others to listen to our transmittals; they have an equal right to our own time and consideration.

As your experience and your expertise as a manager grow, you will find that you are able to get more out of what your peers are sending you with an increasingly smaller expenditure of energy. It will cease to be an obsessive chore, and will become one of the natural tools to which you will turn as a matter of course to get your job done.

Nonverbal Cues and Their Uses

Many of our incoming communications are not associated with sound or the written word. What people *do* in our presence while talking with us is often more revealing than what they say. The alert manager will constantly be making comparisons between these two facets of what is being sent to him.

There are a number of physical activities you should watch for when receiving verbal communications. The first of these is the matter of eye contact. There is an ancient, deeply rooted fallacy that no one can be paying attention to you unless he is looking you in the eye. On the contrary, there are people who can concentrate best on what you are saying when their eyes are closed, and there are others who will fasten their gaze upon your face and be thinking of something entirely different. Your job as the complete communicator is to know your respondents well enough to understand any personal idiosyncracies they may have in the area of eye contact.

Second: Resistance to what is being received is nearly always associated with some bodily activity. There are many of them: foot- or finger-tapping, playing with a pencil, rapid shifting of body positions in the chair, yawning, or a glazing of the eyes. If you are sensitive to these signs, you can usually spot the fact that your input is being badly received. During all of this, verbal responses may be apparently supportive of what you are saying.

Third: Active truculence or hostility may manifest itself nonverbally in many ways not associated with speech. Clenched fists, tight holding of chair arms, tensing of the entire body, reddening of the neck, and even slight bulging of the eyes are dead giveaways that your receiver is actively angry about what he is hearing.

Fourth: There are just as many positive indicators as negative ones. Nodding of the head at frequent intervals, smiling, an alert expression, leaning forward in the chair so as not to miss a word—these usually indicate that your rapport with your listener is complete. One word of caution here: There are some consummate actors who can fake these symbols for reasons of their own. You should be prepared to discount them if they are overdone.

Fifth: The one nearly sure sign that you are getting through to your receiver is a consonance between his speech and his nonverbal cues. If these correspond, you can be relatively sure you are being read, understood, and agreed with. Even so, you must still demand and get later feedback to confirm that judgment.

As managers, we have to remember always how large a part of our work is concerned with the "selling" process. Later, an entire chapter will be devoted to the proliferation of the matrix organization throughout American business and industry. But right now I will simply remark that less and less of our managerial time is being spent in situations where we have complete control. More than half the modern manager's work is done in the role of a coordinator, where people outside his line are keys to the success of his or her work. The art of persuasion is high on the list of skills needed by today's manager.

The good salesman is keenly aware of the dangers of overkill in the selling process. In every situation, there is always an exactly right time to turn off the heat and close the sale; any push beyond this point will have quick and severely negative results. This principle applies to managerial communications as well as to sales. You should closely study both the speech and the nonverbal reactions of your respondent, and when in your opinion he has had enough of the ammunition, stop your transmittal at once.

Nowhere is there greater necessity for sensitivity in this area than in your involvement with group activities. Constant monitoring of the nonverbal cues of the group will tell you more than anything else about what is really going on in the communicative process you are controlling—or *whether* you are controlling it. Naturally, you will want to pay particular attention to the informal leadership of the group, especially if there is high cohesiveness among the members. They may pay more attention to the cues they receive from the informal leader than they do to what you are saying.

Nonverbal cues go both ways, of course. You can, if you try, use your own nonverbal cues effectively in communication. You can often let your bosses, your peers, and your subordinates know—without committing yourself in speech—that you approve or disapprove of what you are getting, and this can be important to the general tone of your interpersonal relationships throughout the organization. The highest form of this art is achieved when you send one message verbally and the opposite one nonverbally, with the latter being the one received and understood by your listener. This is not necessarily as Machiavellian as it may sound. Conditions may simply be such that this apparent hypocrisy is made necessary, and everyone understands what is going on.

It is hard to overemphasize the importance of this critical aspect of the communicative process. Years of constant attention to nonverbal cues are usually required before you can expect to become an expert in evaluating and using them. However, you should not let this discourage you from starting your education on the subject at once and continuing its pursuit religiously. You can never be a completely effective manager without this skill to draw upon.

WHAT DO YOU HEAR FROM OUTSIDE?

Your incoming data flow will not be limited to messages from within the company. Your enterprise is too much an integrated part of the community for there not to be some information coming from it relevant to your operations.

First, one of the most important things you will learn from outsiders is information that you could never get from your own people, especially critical opinions of your management personnel. Your people will tell outsiders things they would not verbalize within the work surroundings. This is a normal human reaction; people have to find a safety valve somewhere for their frustrations, and they wouldn't choose confidantes within the company for fear of endangering their jobs or limiting their opportunity for advancement. It is your responsibility as a manager to remain objective about these items, and to weigh the evidence carefully before coming to a decision on their validity or lack of it. If the criticisms are true, you can then do something about them as expeditiously as possible.

Second, outsiders, because they are impartial observers, can sometimes give suggestions for improvements that would never occur to employees of the company. We are too close to ourselves to see, sometimes, what is perfectly apparent to others. In these cases, you can make a real contribution to your firm by taking action on this sort of information, and implementing any suggestions that have merit. In other words, be sure you are not blinded by NIH ("not invented here").

Third, be alert for information about the community that affects your thinking or operations and that you could never learn internally. Perhaps some company policy has had an unforeseen impact on the surrounding area which has left you and the firm in an unfavorable light, but which is correctable with a little positive action on your part. Detecting this type of fallout, and doing something about it, will have a significant positive effect on your public relations in the community.

Fourth, if your competitors have plants or offices in the same area as your company, listen attentively to outsiders comments about them. Outsiders can discover things about your competitors that you could never learn for yourself. If this seems to flirt dangerously with industrial espionage, so be it. You can be assured that your competition will be doing the same thing to you, and won't hesitate to take advantage of anything they learn that can help them.

As discussed previously, in order for this kind of information to flow regularly in your direction, it will be necessary for you to cultivate deliberately key contacts on the outside, and make use of them on an ongoing basis. Getting what you need from outsiders will require careful selection of contacts and good planning.

This chapter has taken a look at communications coming your way from all directions. If the management above you in the hierarchy is by policy or by choice reticent in giving you the necessary data, you have a right to demand it, in the interests of doing a good job in your area of responsibility. Or, you may find it necessary to learn ways of bypassing roadblocks that occur in the form of individuals.

So far as those reporting to you are concerned, you will have to be certain that you are not guilty of the same kind of blockage mentioned above. If you make the humbling discovery that you are guilty of this error, you must certainly take the necessary corrective steps. You are hamstrung and helpless unless you have a free and open two-way channel of communications with your subordinates.

Your peers will represent some special problems in communication because you are in a naturally competitive situation with them. You know you have to give them the information necessary to function properly; you have the right to demand reciprocity from them. What you learn from your peers will be a measure of your expertise in communicating and in interpersonal relationships in general.

Nonverbal cues and their interpretation are of supreme importance in your communications. With a little practice, you can put to extremely effective use both the cues you receive and those you send.

Lastly, information received from outside can have tremendous impact on your job as a manager. When you learn something valuable from an outsider, put it to work for you at once.

CHAPTER IX

INTERACTING WITH GROUPS

WHEN WE SAY that a manager is one who gets his work done through others, we are implicitly indicating that he or she will be deeply interested in many kinds of groups. It is *group* activity that has made American business and industry what it is today, rather than individual contributions.

WHICH GROUPS INTEREST THE MANAGER?

When thinking about the groups with which he is associated, the manager usually thinks first of his work group—those people for whom he is responsible. This is natural, since it is by their activities and successes that the manager's effectiveness is measured. If this group is functioning smoothly and responding well to the manager's leadership, he actually has nothing fundamental to worry about. However, things being what they are, this is not usually the case—at least not for very long. If it were, there wouldn't be any necessity for the job of a manager at all.

Second, the manager is deeply interested (or at least he should be) in the various small, informal groups that are always present in an organization, especially if they consist of more than eight or ten people. In a sense, the leaders of these groups are the ones who really "run the shop." If they are with him— if the informal group leadership is essentially on the side of the manager—then he has it made. If two or more informal groups are deeply inimical to management, it is another story entirely, and things can get pretty rocky for everyone concerned. Later sections of this chapter will deal with various ways of handling this kind of problem.

√ Third, any member of management has a great interest in the larger segments of the organization—which become increasingly larger until they finally form the aggregate of the entire enterprise. Relationships with these larger groups become either incredibly complex or more and more remote, depending on the company's organizational structure and the philosophy of its executive echelon. In these situations, the manager's role becomes largely that of an interpreter for, or liaison between, his own and the larger groups. The manager must have great expertise in this area if he is to be an effective salesman of "the company" to his own group. Much of the individual employee's lack of identification with the firm is traceable to the inability of the group's manager to enlarge the scope of his employees' thinking to encompass the organization as a whole. His own perspective is of necessity broader than theirs, and he should make every effort to transfer this wider viewpoint to all members of his group, so that in this one area they can act more like peers than supervisors/subordinates.

Fourth, the manager should take an alert and active interest in *outside* groups that contain significant numbers of his people in their membership. By outside groups, I mean those unrelated to the company and also certain ongoing company-sponsored activities, such as hobby clubs and athletic teams. Sharing of membership between the manager and other employees working for him can often greatly enrich his relationships with them. If the boss bowls in a company league alongside some of his people, or if he belongs to a chess club that contains some of his people as members, this introduces a new and humanizing facet into their relationship. This should not be considered a threat to his position of leadership on the job; no reasonable person has any difficulty in compartmentalizing the two differing relationships. What it does do is to make the employees realize that the boss is just as human as they are, and ordinarily a much more satisfying interaction results.

The same results can be achieved by common membership in groups unrelated to the company, such as service clubs, lodges, and churches. The more often the group memberships of supervisor and supervised coincide, the greater will be the chance for a better and more satisfying understanding among all involved. It is almost always true that the better people know one another, the easier it is for them to achieve smooth interpersonal relationships.

Fifth, we should not fail to note that there are several kinds of groups the manager is interested in for his own personal benefit. Trade groups, associations, professional groups for which he is eligible—all can make their contribution to his growth and development into a better manager. Just so long as he maintains a balance and does not let them become too demanding of his time, multimemberships of this kind can only be good.

Our culture has become so incredibly complex in the last

few decades that no person can live a successful life unless
he is an effective member of literally dozens of groups. This
proliferation of membership will continue, rather than lessen,
and of all the minority groups within our civilization, it is
more important that the manager realize this than any other
person within the workforce. This means, of course, an increasingly faster mental and physical life, with the result that
it becomes harder and harder to "stay in condition" in the
same sense that a modern athlete must. But it is just as necessary for the manager as for the professional football player.
It is a major tragedy that so few of our universities and schools
of business have as yet recognized this aspect of the new breed
of manager. In effect, we are still trying to throw most of
our new members of management out into the middle of the
pond to see whether they can swim back, without giving them
any previous instructions on *how* to swim. It is not only bar-
baric but terribly wasteful of some of our finest managerial
potential, for many young managers become disgusted and
leave the field because of this fact.

Ways of Approaching Groups

There are, of course, as many ways for an individual to approach different groups as there are people themselves—actually, several times as many, because each of us, if we are
smart, will use varying kinds of approaches for varying groups.
Here, however, we will limit ourselves to the ways in which
a manager approaches four types of groups in which he has
an interest.

First: You will always be under the necessity of approaching the management group above you in the hierarchy. It
should be noted that in all likelihood you will not approach

this *group* in the same way that you make contact with your own immediate manager. Your relationship with this person will usually be much easier and closer than the relationships you attain with his peers or those above him. When you have occasion to initiate contact with the group above you, it is usually to do a selling job (make a presentation). The one unalterable sine qua non for this situation is to have done your homework impeccably. Be prepared to defend yourself vigorously against any possible sniping—and there will usually be some—but do it in such a way as to avoid arousing their irritation or hostility. The key here is to maintain an unfailing and obvious air of objectivity. You—and they—are concerned above all with the facts relevant to the question at hand.

Second: Your peer *group* is naturally a different entity than any one of the individuals comprising it. Here you have certain inherent rights and privileges simply because this is *your* group. You can defend them as vigorously as is consonant with your personality and as seems advisable in the situation. I have already mentioned some of the limitations inherent in your relationships with your peers because of the competition that exists naturally among you, but try to minimize the inhibitory effect of this competition. Keep exchanges with your peer group as open and free as you can, even if it means going an extra step once in a while. You won't be the loser if you do this; they will be the losers if they don't try it themselves sometimes.

Third: The group that reports to you is by all odds the most critical one to your present and future success, and you should take more care with this than with any other business group you have contact with. Above all, you should never give even the *appearance* of being condescending or patronizing. It is much easier to fall into this trap than one might think at first. Even when it arises out of the everyday business of your job, apparent abstraction or lack of complete contact with your group can do irreparable harm to your rapport with them. The way to avoid this trap is consciously to cultivate the ability to concentrate totally on the business at hand, *and then show that you are doing so.* Just as a lack of attention to a group of your people is the greatest insult you can give them, so the greatest compliment is to indicate in all ways that they are the center of your universe during a group meeting. This means, of course, that every member of the group should be recognized when he asks to be, and that everyone's inputs should be given equal consideration. Your people will judge your fairness partly by how you conduct yourself in these situations, and they won't hesitate to express their judgments to each other.

There are, naturally, several kinds of group meetings you might call for your subordinates, and you will probably develop different kinds of roles for different occasions. The climate in a meeting on safety, for example, is quite different from that in a meeting where you are considering a production problem. If you are having a group meeting for consideration of employees' suggestions, still another mien would be appropriate. In any event, it is highly important to be *consistent* in the differing roles required of you in the several kinds of meetings you will find necessary to call. Here is one situation where predictability on the part of the boss is a major virtue. Employees don't like to have to "second guess" what their boss's mood and approach will be from time to time in the same kinds of meetings. When you have identified the most functional approach in a given scene, stick to it like glue in future events of the same kind.

Fourth: Your approaches to informal groups outside the work milieu will be even more varied. In many cases, you will want to cultivate seriously a "nonboss" attitude. If you and your employees have common memberships in hobby groups, for example, make them realize that you consider them at least your equal. Nowhere would it be more deadly to "pull rank" than in this situation. You would immediately become an isolate if they spotted this in your behavior.

To generalize: The approach to the informal group is in most cases just that—informality. The lower-keyed you can keep your entry into the group, the greater your acceptance will be, and the greater your chance for a successful group interaction. In these situations you should concentrate on the contribution *you* can make to the group, not on what the group can do for you.

Finally, and of great import, study each group with which you have contact as a separate entity. Groups, like individuals, have personalities, and you must get to know these personalities well before you can have an enriching interaction with them.

Reading Group Reactions

Whatever efforts you make to communicate with the group will be in vain unless you learn sensitivity in reading group reactions. In a majority of cases on the business scene, the group will not verbalize—at least not clearly—what their reaction is to an action or a communication from you. You are going to have to be dependent on other methods of understanding what they are thinking.

In reading the reactions of your own work group, there are a number of points to keep in mind. First: Positive reactions to your transmittal are much more likely to be expressed verbally than negative ones. All of us would ordinarily rather be the bearers of good news than of bad. When you have communicated something to the group that pleases them, their tendency will be to tell you so. A negative reaction from the group is always bad news to the manager.

Second: A sudden cutoff of what has been a good flow of incoming data from the group is a negative sign. If their habit has been to be fairly free and easy with you, and this pattern is suddenly negated, you can be quite sure that the group has received a signal which either displeases or threatens them. They will fall back to examine internally what the signal means to them before they will return to something like normal communications with you. If their final verdict is negative, you can expect certain "normal" reactions to this: production slowdowns, quality problems, increase in complaints and grievances, perhaps even a worsened safety record, if your group is engaged in manufacturing. Remember, a pattern of these things is more likely to be a series of symptoms, rather than the disease itself. This is your signal to do a little intensive investigation to determine the cause of the group's malaise.

Third: A sharp increase in the group's cohesiveness accompanied simultaneously by an apparent isolation of you, the manager, from the group is a strong indicator that the members consider themselves severely threatened. When group intracommunication proliferates and outgoing signals are diminished, you have one of the clearest indicators of serious problems within your group. There is always the off chance that the group is trying to protect you from something they know that you don't, but this is rare. It is far more probable that they consider you to be the causative agent of their discomfiture. Now is the time to bore in hard on the informal leadership of your group to find out what is going on that you don't know about. You should persevere in this investigation even if you suspect you may discover something highly disturbing.

Fourth: On the positive side, be alert for indicators that group morale is on the upswing. If the flow of suggestions has been sluggish and you notice a significant rise in the number of them being offered, it is probable that you have done something, or a series of things, which have been received well by your group. Or, again, there may be an upward trend of the indicators mentioned a moment ago: greater production volume, better quality, reduction of grievances, and an improved safety index.

As a manager, you must avoid the danger of tunnel vision. Too much concentration on your group alone can be misleading. It is only when you put into perspective the behavior of your group as compared to other groups around it that you have a decent chance of seeing the whole picture. This means that you must maintain your pipelines into groups other than your own, and take regular readings of their behavior. Check frequently with your peers as to conditions in their groups; compare notes freely in order to determine what the trends are in the entire organization. If you discover, after noting danger signals in your group, that others are experiencing the same thing, at least you are no worse off than they are. But if you see red flags and your peers report only green lights and clear tracks, you are then in a situation that demands immediate remedial activity. This is the time to confer freely with the management above you, and to get as many inputs as you can from any sophisticated observers.

If your rapport and communication with your group have been seriously damaged, for whatever reason, you must bear the major charge of taking remedial steps. Don't expect the group to initiate action, except in the most unusual cases. They consider—and rightly—that you as the manager carry the heavier responsibility here, just as you do in so many other facets of your job.

Learning to read group reactions is just exactly what the term indicates: learning to *read*. As a child (depending upon the educational philosophy of your school administration), you first learned the alphabet, then started to recognize how individual letters are combined into words, then into phrases, then sentences, then paragraphs, and then longer connected sequences. Learning to read group reactions is likewise a step-by-step process, in which you become increasingly sophisticated as you go. When you became a manager, there is a good chance that you had not consciously thought of the necessity of being sensitive to the actions of the group. Everyone *is*, in his own way, but this sensitivity must become a conscious skill and an integral part of your job.

Achieving expertise in interpreting group reactions is, like so many other facets of your work, a matter of establishing a new habit. You must first acquire a mental set conducive to increased perceptivity and accurate methods of analysis. From then on, you practice, practice, practice, until you have conditioned yourself to be alert for any changes in the group climate. And alertness in interpreting group reactions is a primary requisite for smooth operation in any managerial job.

The Manager and Informal Leadership

I have already mentioned several times the relationships between the manager and the informal leadership of his work group, but this relationship should be brought into sharper focus. The kinds of rapport, or lack of it, that the manager has with the informal leadership will in large measure determine his overall effectiveness as the group's formal leader—the boss.

The most important result of having a good relationship is that the amount of persuasive and even corrective "people" work the manager is required to do will be significantly reduced. If you, the manager, have informal leadership going your way, the rest of the group will be with you also, with little or no effort on your part to sell individuals on your objectives.

Informal leadership depends entirely for its effectiveness on internal authority, and, in the final analysis, this is the only truly viable way to run the ship. You as manager have nominal authority, of course, and can at any time veto the decisions of the informal leadership—on paper. Your goal naturally will be to acquire internal authority as well as positional authority, and this highly desirable result occurs when you and the informal leadership are working in consonance toward the same general goals. It would, perhaps, be a trifle naive to assume that there could ever be *perfect* accord between the two of you, but there can be enough accord to visibly enhance the overall achievements of the group.

There are two steps you must take before you can move toward this goal. First, you must *identify* the informal leadership in the various subgroups, and this is not always as easy to do as it sounds. Some individuals prefer to operate as "cryptoleaders," feeling that their effectiveness will be increased because they are not under public scrutiny from management. Thus it is entirely possible to have a "shadow" informal organization set up within your group, in which the apparent leader is a "straw man" whose puppet strings are under the control of another person. It is up to you as a sentient manager to be able to ferret out this situation, and to identify positively the person with whom you are going to have to come to grips.

The other step in preparing for positive action is to study the informal leader to the point where you can predict his or her actions with a high degree of certainty. At the same time, it is imperative that the informal leader be allowed to come to know you just as well as you know him. It must be a mutual affair before it can be functional. Again, it is not necessary for friendship to exist between the two of you—only understanding. This understanding must be coupled with a belief, on both your parts, that it will be advantageous for all concerned that you work together to achieve the organization's objectives.

Direct confrontation between you and informal leadership can bring the entire machinery of your organization to a screeching halt. When the influence of the informal leadership is against you, your work will be multiplied to an almost impossible degree. You are then required to go back to a one-to-one effort with every member of your group, and this is so time-consuming that you will be hopelessly bogged down in persuasion of individuals and in putting out the many brush fires that will arise in this situation.

The situation just described is not *entirely* hopeless, however. Remember, your people will be keeping continuous surveillance of the obvious struggle going on between you and the informal leadership, and at the particular moment the group decides that you are the stronger of the two in leadership qualities, the informal leader will be deposed—dumped unceremoniously. Naturally, this void will soon be filled by another person or persons, and you will then have to undergo the preliminary skirmishing again. The plural "persons" was used because informal leadership in groups is often *rotational* in nature. That is, the group, as it identifies the particular strengths of its members, will choose different informal leaders to perform different functions. If your reporting organization is medium sized or large, an imposing number of people may comprise the subgroup we call informal leadership.

Another intervening variable that can complicate your managerial life is the existence of rivalries among the membership of the informal leadership. When schisms, factionalism, or splinter groups form, they can cause you trouble on a major scale. In this situation you will find a significant amount of your managerial time devoted to throwing oil on the troubled organizational sea.

The important thing is for you, the manager, to be aware of these basic facts of group life, and to be mentally prepared to spend the time and effort entailed in controlling them.

There are, of course, some mechanical methods of controlling informal leadership. To take care of emergent problems, you may have to consider changing informal leaders' job assignments, moving them to other locations, or perhaps even transferring them to other departments. But these should be considered last resorts.

PREDICTIONS DOWNSTREAM

The ultimate purpose of the manager's attention to his relationships with groups is to be able to make predictions about what the group will do in a given set of circumstances, especially in relation to their estimates of his leadership abilities. The manager should be especially sensitive in the area of proposed new-policy declaration. He should be able to prognosticate with a great deal of accuracy how his people will react to a change in operational procedure resulting from a new policy. Moreover, it is the clear and evident duty of the manager to inform his group if he feels that the proposed policy will have a negative effect on their activities. This, naturally, ties directly back to the amount and quality of the communications up and down the entire hierarchy of management. If these communications are good, there is a relatively large chance that ill-considered policy can be headed off at the pass and a massacre avoided.

The manager must also be sophisticated in his ability to forecast what sorts of things his group might be expected to initiate on their own, either positive or negative in nature. This will be conditioned by the group itself, by the nature and personality of the manager, and by outside variables over which no one in the group has any measure of control. This means that the manager must use his wider sources of information, and his access to people with expertise in various fields, to make predictions about possible combinations of these variables. In other words, his planning must be extensive and imaginative. For any combination of variables, he should have several alternative plans in mind, and his mental set should be flexible enough to enable him to adjust to any quick change in the picture. It is this sort of maneuverability that will be make or break for the success of the group's activities.

In doing this sort of planning, the manager must at all times be highly conscious of his level of operations. First, second, and even third levels of management make very short-range plans and decisions. They must be thinking in terms of today, next week, or a month or two. The decision-making processes of middle managers generally cover six months to two years. The executive echelon makes its predictions and decisions in terms of years, with the chief executive absorbed in what is going to happen to the enterprise five or ten years from now.

It is inevitable, of course, that it will sometimes be necessary to make downstream predictions about certain key *individuals*, as well as the group at large. Because of special influence they may exert on the group, or because of the kinds of interactions taking place between them and you, this kind of one-on-one thinking becomes imperative. Nor should you overlook the ramifications that their future actions will have for the group at large. The general effect is a series of nonconcentric circles that form a complex maze of tangencies and overlappings. All in all, it makes for an interesting sort of mental life.

Not to be forgotten for a moment is the continuing necessity for you to communicate your thinking to those above you in the line. Fortunately or unfortunately, according to your expertise in this area, you must put yourself on record many times a month with your managers and their peers. They depend heavily on this sort of input coming up to condition their own thinking and planning. The fact that you will be building a book for yourself in the minds of upper management must not become inhibitory to this necessary part of your everyday job. One sure way to commit managerial suicide is to fail to go through with this process. A blank record in this area is an automatic indication of your abdication of managerial responsibility. It is far better to be wrong in a few predictions than not to have made any at all.

Remember that you have a multitude of resources to help you in making these predictions. The most useful resource of all is the members of your own group. When you have good rapport with them, you should never hesitate to discuss with them the possible actions you are considering. It may be valuable to get their individual and group reactions before making your own decision about a particular case.

In a sense, this chapter has been a synthesis of some of the elements of the manager's interpersonal relationships that were discussed previously. There are a number of groups in which the manager is vitally interested: his own work group, the larger groups that comprise the entire firm or agency, the peer groups of other managers, and outside groups that have a tangential connection with his operations. You must become intimately familiar with the workings of all these groups to be effective.

The alert manager will vary his approach to different groups according to their composition, their relationships to him, and the overall situation. As a manager, you must become extremely expert in reading group reactions to all varieties and combinations of circumstances. Most of the cues you receive here will be nonverbal in nature, especially if the group's reactions are neutral or negative.

Another highly important consideration is the relationships you have with the informal leadership of groups. Whether these relationships are positive or negative will grossly affect your managerial effectiveness.

Finally, a careful evaluation of all the above elements will improve your ability to bat well in making predictions about group reactions downstream. The better you are at predicting these reactions, the more you will be able to control them positively toward the betterment of the health of the entire organization.

CHAPTER X

BUILDING THE TEAM

THE LAST CHAPTER was concerned with the manager's relationships with groups of various sorts. This one will focus on a special kind of group: the team. More and more these days we are coming to realize that in our modern scene a simple *group* cannot get the job done. A team is characterized by particular relationships and interactions that go beyond the simpler definition of the group.

TEAM RELATIONSHIPS

A group is defined as two or more persons with common goals or objectives. The operational definition of a team is much harder to come by, because the word means different things to different managers, depending on their level of sophistication, the kinds of people they have working for them, and the sort of work being done. The Theory X manager has a team—a team of slaves over whom he cracks the whip as they toil endlessly. The 9,9 manager on the Blake-Mouton Managerial Grid® is a team manager also—one who leads a team of people who are actively and perhaps even eagerly cooperating in the development of a method to attain their common goals. Between these two extremes there falls an almost infinite variety of other conceptualizations of what a team should be. Our goal here is to examine the kinds of relationships that are common to almost all kinds of teams.

First: In the more simply defined "group," the members do indeed have common goals, but it is possible for individuals within the group to more or less go their own ways, and to work as individual contributors if they so wish. Not so in the team. The first requisite of team membership is that everyone involved recognize the absolute necessity of cooperation with every other member of the team. No one can be allowed the luxury of pure self-determination; the primary considerations are deciding what is best for the team and finding the best and most equitable distribution of the work load.

Second: All of us are human beings, but it is vital to the success of the team that individual personality differences be buried six feet deep when the work is under way. Under the pressures of team work, there is simply no time for wheel-spinning or repairing of interpersonal abrasions. This is why the wise manager will take whatever time is necessary to pick the team members who best fit the criteria he has decided on. Better to delay the start of a project until the team membership is ideal than to have the whole thing go down the drain because of improper selection of personnel. This can be frustrating to a manager who is used to "charging" at his goals; he should repress unmercifully any tendency he has to make compromises simply to get the show on the road.

Third: It is incumbent on any member of a team to be supportive of the rest of the membership to the fullest extent of his ability—and beyond it. This is not as self-sacrificing as it sounds, for serving as a member of a team should result in personal growth in the ability to give aid and comfort to the rest of the members. It should be noted that a true team exhibits more synergy than does the common garden variety of group. (Synergy is defined as the evidence that the actions of a group are greater than the total of the individual contributions made by the members.) We get "more for our money" from a team than a nonteam group.

Fourth: Also implicit in team membership is the willingness to subordinate self-interest to a far greater extent than many of us have been used to doing before. The members must feel involved in a true *community of effort* before team membership can be achieved in the fullest sense of the words. When Wilt Chamberlain became a team player, the Los Angeles Lakers literally blew apart the National Basketball Association. Or, to reverse the coin, in any given sport nearly everyone knows of some championship team that truly had no "stars."

Fifth: Team membership demands a continuing flexibility on the part of the members. Changing conditions require frequent realignment of smaller working groups within the team. Just when one has grown truly comfortable in working with two or three other people, the new job will necessitate a reassignment with others whom he does not know as well—yet.

Sixth: Cohesiveness of the team will be significantly higher *at all times* than in the average group. It will not take an external or internal threat to group security to draw the members together. But such a threat can result in an even greater degree of cohesiveness. (A good team, for example, is always subject to threats from jealous competitors outside.)

Seventh: the objectivity demanded of the team far tran-scends that demanded of other kinds of groups. You must be prepared to take criticism of the roughest sort if your performance is judged to be dysfunctional by the other members or the leader. The saving grace of this situation is that the criticism will be rendered on an impersonal basis: It's not *you* that's being criticized, but your *actions*. In this context, there is no necessity for a defensive posture on your part. Change your course in consonance with that of the skipper and the rest of the crew, and the matter will be forgotten.

These days, not everyone has the capability, or even the desire, to become a good team member. That is why the day of the entrepreneur will never come to an end. The requirements of team membership as outlined above are indeed rigorous, and the last of the rugged individualists among us give team membership the ugly label of "regimentation." For those with a propensity toward team membership, this is not so; they think of it as a method of self-actualization not realizable elsewhere in the work arena. We are lucky these differences exist, for we need both sorts of people to make up a balanced business world.

THE MANAGER AND THE STRONG TEAM

It would, of course, be too great a generalization to say that no strong team has ever been developed without strong leader-ship, but the odds are astronomically against such an occurrence. There is no single prescription for good team leadership; managers who are successful in this area display a wide variety of leadership styles.

For example, a task-oriented manager zeroes in on "getting the job done" until the faces of the people before him fade from view. To him, they are not really people. But he does get the job done, and the merchandise out on the loading dock on time. For this he is respected by his managers, and sometimes even by his people. He often develops a strong team: strong in production, and strong and united in their dislike of or hatred for their leader. This situation is hardly desirable in these days when employees have so much more mobility than they did in years past. The visible and invisible costs of high turnover are among the worst profit-robbers known.

The "middle of the road" manager can be the catalyst for the growth of a strong team, too. His favorite word is "compromise," and he is likely to turn to this device for the settlement of any controversy that arises among the members of his team. This man or woman will strive for an equal, but not necessarily maximal, balance between attention to the task and care for his people—who, by the way, are very real to him. It is very likely that this manager will be referred to as an "old pro" by his peers, since he has an obvious ability to survive and in most management circles would be considered an unqualified success. Incidentally, this very human tendency to compromise is found frequently among the members of middle management, because of the intense pressures to which they are subjected from above, from below, and from all sides.

The true "team manager" is the one who is maximally concerned with *both* the task and the people on his crew. He tends to confront his problems head-on and fight them out to a finish. When policy or procedure debates arise in his group, someone usually wins and someone usually loses, but the decision gets made—on the basis of the best facts available—and the job gets done. Because this type of leader is so patently sincere and objective, few battle wounds are incurred by his team members, and those that *are* incurred heal quickly and leave no scars. This leader is charismatic, and his team members are so glad to be with him that they don't mind a few bumps and abrasions, just so long as they get to go on the ride. It's a heady experience.

Thus several types of leadership styles may be employed to come up with a strong team, but the fact remains that the leadership itself, in some form or another, is mandatory for the welding of any real team. Good teams don't just grow like weeds. One of the attributes always found in a strong team manager is his ability to communicate. In this area, he must have even higher standards than other types of managers. The leader must transmit far more efficiently than other, lower-level managers; he must receive and interpret quickly and accurately; he must demand and give clear, succinct, and understandable feedback so that the loop is always properly closed. The good team leader will also possess a greater-than-average amount of the reciprocal skill: He will be a listener par excellence. He will make of listening a positive, recognizable, and comfortable part of his managerial armament, so that his people will always know they can communicate with him with total assurance of getting a fair hearing. Once such an atmosphere is established, the noes necessary now and then are much less unpalatable than when they are viewed as whimsical or ill-considered.

Actually, these aspects of the team leader's ability are only one facet of a larger and more inclusive attribute: his or her ability to be *supportive* of team members under any and all conditions—even up to and including the inevitable failures that are bound to occur in either individual or team performance. The loss of one skirmish has almost never decided the outcome of a war. The supportive team leader must give continual good coaching to his members and must seize every opportunity to turn a mistake or setback into a learning experience. It is an odd quirk of human nature that we can often learn better from our mistakes than from our successes, because many of the latter happen fortuitously.

Because he has several traits in greater amounts than other managers, the team leader is going to have more respect and confidence from his team members than other types of managers enjoy. The members of a team will be more than willing to recognize strong management when it is demonstrated, and their attitudes will serve to perpetuate the success of the enterprise. Winners form the habit of winning, just as some unfortunates form the habit of losing and are almost uncomfortable if by accident they happen to win.

The mental set of the team leader is different from that of the "average" manager. He realizes fully that his way of life is more precarious than that of the manager who decides to play it safe and just make sure no glaring errors are committed. The team manager is willing to take high risks for the chances of reaping high rewards. Many a team leader has committed his whole future to a project when the chances for success were only a fraction greater than 50 percent. Yet to call him a gambler is not really doing justice to the team manager either, since he will have done his homework impeccably before setting the engine in motion, and most certainly he will have left no *controllable* variables to chance.

Maintaining Control

If you, the manager, have done a good job of selecting the personnel for your team, you will thereby have built in some problems for yourself. If this sounds contradictory, so be it. The analogy between the team and the growing boy is not too bad a one. A normal, healthy American boy is one of the most difficult things in the world to control, and so is a normal, healthy American work team. Both have so much boundless energy, curiosity, aggressiveness, and ambition that they are hard to curb. Nor would you want to curb them entirely. By so doing, you would negate the very purpose for building the team in the first place.

There are some steps you can take, however, that will help you to keep the team operating within a reasonable sphere of activity, which is what you are after. First: Don't lose control in the first place. Before you get too turned off by this seemingly simplistic statement, stop and think for a moment. You *are* in control at the outset. You pick the team membership; you state and reinforce the objectives the team has to reach; you have a large measure of control over the methodology you are going to employ to get there. These important factors, plus your nominal leadership position and whatever charisma and inner authority you have going for you, are enough to do the job—if you keep them in balance.

Second: Get quick and total involvement from every member of the team. Since this process will be examined in the next section of this chapter, I will only mention it briefly here.

Third: Reassure yourself that your objectives are clearly and completely understood by everyone on the team. It is easy to assume that they are as crystal clear to your team members as they are to you, but this assumption may well be fallacious. You will need to evoke your best skills as a communicator to make certain that everyone is looking in the same direction toward the same targets. More frustrations arise from misunderstandings in this area than in any other facet of team efforts. Reassurance on this point is worth whatever time it takes to get it.

There is another advantage to the above approach: A thoroughgoing discussion by the team during the initial stages of the project may well result in altering or expanding the objectives. It is entirely possible that their inputs will suggest things you overlooked before that will have a significant impact on the job. It's a poor team leader who is unable to learn from his group because of false pride or a failure to recognize merit when he sees it.

Fourth: Rely on the help of the informal leadership of your team. We have been down this road before, so all I will do here is remind you of how useful these people can be if you handle them correctly. And, unfortunately, how stultifying their actions can be if they are *not* in harmony with your intentions.

Fifth: Take great care in the assignment of individual work loads. The effectiveness you display here is a function of how well you understand your people as individuals, and it is starry-eyed nonsense to expect that every member of the team will make an equal contribution. People just are not equally endowed, and this is one of the first things the team leader has to understand and allow for.

While on the topic of control, we should also give a thought to the numbers and kinds of specific controls set up for the operation of a team. Generally, the fewer the better, but it would be naive to suppose that any work group could be put together where there would be no necessity for checks and measurements of the team's progress toward its goals. Once more, the numbers and kinds of controls you as a team leader decide to use will be conditioned by both your personnel and the situation itself. One of the most important factors, of course, is the nature of the task you are performing. If your team is engaged in the manufacture of some fairly simple children's toys, it is logical that you would need few controls; if your team is working in aerospacecraft, where immensely complicated construction and absolute reliability are imperative, you could well have a thick book of minutely detailed controls.

To say that controlling the team is essential to successful leadership is a true statement, but it is not the whole truth. For certain psychological reasons, control of a strong work team is many times more difficult than control of a more heterogeneous work group. However, there are a number of things working in your favor. At the outset, the individuals on your team will be more highly motivated than the members of lesser groups. There will also be more ego involvement, because they have been specially chosen to enter the team. Commitment to the team—and hopefully to you, the team manager—will be deep. This combination of vectors will almost certainly result in your members' making greater efforts, and mobilizing much more energy, than the workers on lesser jobs. The last thing in the world you want to do is to reduce this energy flow; your intent, and job as a team manager, is to channel it down the most productive road toward the achievement of your team goals.

There are so many references in management literature to the "challenge of leadership" that the expression is in danger of becoming a cliché. Yet the simple, enduring truth remains that the manager's job *is* a challenging one, and is becoming increasingly so almost daily. No facet of management is more heavily or directly challenging than the necessity for maintaining proper control over the membership of your team. Once again, it's your ball game; go play it.

GETTING PARTICIPATION

So far in this chapter, there has been an implication that the members of every team had been anxiously awaiting appointment to it and are eager to go charging off into battle. This is not always strictly true. Some teams are built by design; some evolve slowly under a developing leadership; some happen more or less fortuitously under a combination of circumstances. In the latter two cases especially, it is the job of the team manager to elicit, by whatever means he has at his command, full participation of all the team members.

There are several facets to the manager's planning in this area. One of the more important ones is to assure himself that he has made proper work assignments. The team members should be put into the juxtapositions that are most conducive to drawing the best efforts from all individuals. Sometimes this is done by putting friends into the same pairings or small team groups; here you are depending on already present good will to help escalate the efforts. Sometimes you may make a calculated decision to pair not friends, but natural rivals, so that competition can become a significant factor in stimulating productivity. This particular gambit must be scrutinized closely and continually to see that it doesn't get out of hand, but it may be productive if properly managed. Small groups within the larger team can be handled in similar fashion, often with advantages to the entire group effort. Even in teams that evolve gradually, with minimal planning, the manager has a responsibility to recognize the slow formation of a team, observe its growth and development, and make work assignments accordingly.

Nowhere is there better opportunity for a canny use of job enrichment than in the management of a team. In fact, this technique can be the key to the success of an entire project, if the team manager can coax the upper echelons into cooperating with his plans for enlarging individual and team responsibilities. When successful, job enrichment in the team will have spectacular results. There will be a vastly increased sense of fulfillment for both individuals and small groups within the team; production and quality will both be improved; and, because of the high visibility of the successful results, the people involved will have a greater chance for recognition and personal advancement than they would in a more static or less imaginative job situation.

No manager should ever be above using personal influence and the loyalties of his team members to bring about a betterment of their performance. "Doing it for the coach" has won countless athletic championships; the same thing can occur in an industrial or business situation. It has already been pointed out that good team leaders are charismatic. If we possess this rare characteristic, we should be less than normally bright if we did not take advantage of every ounce of it in getting our team members to extend themselves to their fullest.

The display of a good measure of decisiveness on the part of the team manager will have a salutary effect on the team's overall achievements. They *want* positive leaders who know where they're going and how to get there. This is not to say that the followership of the team should be mindless or blind. It is just that team members are more content when they have evidence that their leadership is strong and effective. Obviously, no one but the leader can give this evidence, and it must be unmistakable to everyone.

The team manager must be a little further down the road ahead of his fellows than is true of the conventional types of work-group leaders. He may feel the lonelier for it, but he has to be far enough out in front of his troops that his innovations and broader perspective are incontrovertible. This is the underlying reason for my earlier statement that the team leader must be prepared to take larger risks than his more humdrum peers. He will not always be right; his overall goal is for his successes to materially outweigh his failures, in both numbers and importance to the project.

It was mentioned earlier that the team leader may sometimes introduce competitiveness into the team situation. But his concern with competition is not just limited to the intramural. Competition with other teams arises frequently, as when two teams are aiming at the same prize or one team directly challenges another. Physically, the first sensing of a competitive situation stimulates the flow of our adrenalin and sharpens our natural senses. However, these reactions vary widely from person to person, and the team manager is going to have to judge carefully the strength of the competitive spirit among his various team members. You can't afford many mistakes here, because too much of your total success is riding on the individual judgments you make about the effects of competition on each person under your guidance. Hand in hand with these judgments go others that will tell you when to relax the pressure on one person while increasing it on another. A coach's ability to juggle the available number of "time outs" is crucial to the outcome of a game. This is as true for smaller groups within the team as it is for the individual members of it.

In summary, the reasons for getting full participation will be self-evident to any alert manager. There is much more to the operation of a true team than simply going through routine motions, such as suffice in more mundane types of working organizations. The good team has great potential: Both its leaders and its members are of much higher caliber than is found in the usual work group.

MANIPULATION OR DEVELOPMENT?

There is much confusion in the thinking of managerial people at all levels concerning the real core of the manager's job: What should be his *real* relationship with his people? On the positive side, leaders in business have gradually come to believe that it is part of their duty to tend to the development and growth of those who report to them. This much any person can accept with equanimity—even with a tiny glow of satisfaction that he may have contributed to the personal or professional growth of his subordinates. If the manager, through his longer experience and wider knowledge, can be of help in pointing out areas where a junior employee can enhance his strengths or neutralize his weaknesses, he has rendered him a real service. If the manager can help by establishing a climate for growth, or perhaps by actually furnishing some of the tools whereby the employee can improve himself, then managerial euphoria is increased significantly. Helping others, even if it is a necessity because of our position in the business hierarchy, is a satisfying and enjoyable experience.

It is on the obverse side of the coin that the traumas and hangups appear. Any thinking manager, by reading the position description accompanying his job, cannot escape the fact that he has a clearly delineated responsibility to direct and control the actions of those people reporting to him. His own managers make this crystal clear and inescapable. In other words, implicit in the position description of a manager is the necessity for him to *manipulate* his people. And this realization terrifies him, unless his nature is truly Machiavellian, because an aura of opprobrium has grown up around the word "manipulation" until it has become a first-class insult to tell people they are manipulators.

Whether a particular manager deserves the bad connotations that go with this depends entirely on his motives as he performs this part of his duties. If the manager manipulates his people solely to accomplish something for his own personal gain, he is indeed a moral reprobate and should get all the sanctions that a group normally imposes for this kind of action. It is never defensible to use others for one's own aggrandizement without their knowledge and support. Unfortunately, this is what the word "manipulation" means to most people. But there is another, largely forgotten meaning of the term: "managing or handling directed toward some object."* Manipulation can be not only moral but even altruistic. When the boss directs his efforts solely toward the good of the group as a whole and all the members benefit from his actions, the manager is simply doing his job. He is accomplishing the charge that has been laid upon him by his own management, and no one can successfully fault him for this kind of activity.

Thus the team leader must become quite adept at balancing two sorts of directive actions: direction, whereby work assignments and the controls put upon them are determined

* *Webster's Third New International Dictionary.*

by the leader and communicated to the members of the team; and stimulation for growth and development of the team members, by being supportive and exercising a real and positive leadership evident to and appreciated by all the group. The desired outcomes include the attainment of the team's objective, the growth and development of the team's members, and further maturation and gaining of greater expertise by the team leader. These are the most salutary results of the formation and development of a working team.

This chapter has approached the team concept from several angles. First, we analyzed some of the characteristics of team relationships that set them apart from other work groups. The true team is several cuts above the type of group that has traditionally been common on the American industrial scene; it takes a little doing for the manager in charge of a team to enlarge his perspective. In most cases the leader, to remain successful, will have to be able to grow faster than the members he has chosen for his team, and this requires personal outputs not known before in his managerial career.

Any manager who has been picked to develop a team should have only one personal ambition: to make it a strong and winning team. This will entail learning several new things for himself as well as directing the crew. New work habits must be inculcated and developed; new performance norms will have to be established.

Because he will have sought out and admitted superior types of workers to his team, the manager will find it harder to maintain control of a strong team than of one of the older, less dynamic work groups. His operation will be best when he keeps the number of controls to a minimum but chooses them carefully and sees to it that they do the job for which they were designed.

Finally, a distinction was made between the inspirational (developmental) side of the team manager's job, and the more mundane directional efforts he must make in order to manipulate his people in a positive manner.

CHAPTER XI

RELATIONSHIPS IN
THE MATRIX ORGANIZATION

THERE CAN BE little question that the shape of American business and industry is changing rapidly, and that the change will continue at an even faster rate in the near future. The older styles of organizational structure—such as the scalar (or pyramidal), functional, and geographic structures—simply are no longer functional for the increasing complexity of American commerce. We are seeing more and more leading companies turn to the *matrix* organization, simply because it gets the job done with less strain and with more efficiency than was possible under the traditional structures. In the matrix there is still a line relationship within one discipline, but the basic concept is that the discipline *must be responsive to every other part of the total organization upon call.*

Take, for example, the engineering department of a medium-sized firm. Under the old concept, the engineers would pursue a compartmentalized activity, subject only to the direction and leadership of their department head and the executive echelon in the company. In a matrix organization, engineering would still be doing some independent work, but they would be ready to respond to the needs and problems of any other discipline or function within the firm. While they were working on a given assignment from, say, manufacturing, the engineers assigned to this project would report *only* to manufacturing management. In every respect, they would be responsible to manufacturing for their work and its results.

RECONDITIONING THE MANAGER

If a firm changes over to the matrix form of organization and the supervisors and management involved have had any length of experience under an older form of organization, some major reorienting and reconditioning must be done with the thinking of these managers. In some respects, the change will amount to a 180-degree turnaround.

First: Gone forever will be the old, set-in-concrete law of "one man, one boss." Ever since the first writings on management, theoreticians have assumed as incontrovertible that it is a vile sin against principle to have "dual" or "multiple" supervision of a workman. The psychological justification for this was the idea that the subordinate would experience too much trauma and uncertainty about what to do first, what system of priorities to follow. In a sense, this is still a problem (and will be dealt with as such in a later section of this chapter). But what is really involved here is making the manager aware that he must be responsible to many different superiors *one at a time*, and that he can no longer attach himself permanently to one boss for the rest of his working life in a given organization. It is essential that the manager accept wholeheartedly the idea that he can and will be responsive to many other managers when he is working on a project of theirs. Sometimes it will even happen that the manager will find himself splitting his available time between two or more jobs simultaneously. The often repeated guidepost along this new managerial road is *flexibility*.

Second: Another thing that used to be a cardinal sin to the management theorist is now becoming commonplace in the matrix organization: an inversion of leadership. The follower in one task force may become the leader (over his former boss) in the next project, simply because he possesses greater expertise in the new venture. (This subject will also be covered more fully later in this chapter.)

Third: No matrix organization can ever hope to be successful unless it throws itself bodily into the life of continuing team membership. This follows logically from the advantages of team membership outlined in the preceding chapter. The difference is that in a matrix organization the manager will find himself successively in many different teams doing many different kinds of tasks under many different leaderships. This brings up a possible danger: It may result in a continuing impermanence of interpersonal relationships that will have a serious effect on the mental health of some individuals. It may, in fact, cause symptoms like those present in the behavior of children raised by parents who traveled continually and lived in a series of hotels. This syndrome should be watched for carefully by all managers, and if it is spotted an effort should be made to introduce more permanence into the work situation of the subordinate in question. If there is anything this country does *not* need, it is a proliferation of such transient interpersonal relationships that no one feels he has any real roots.

It is logical (and correct) to assume that the easiest way to enter a matrix organization is at the inception of the enterprise. If you are beginning an enterprise and have decided a matrix organization is best, start it that way, and staff it with management and workers who have either had experience in matrices before or who give evidence of easy adaptability to the concept. If this cannot be done, but the exigencies of the present environment seem to dictate a reorganization into a matrix from one of the older forms, then an extensive and intensive retraining job should be done with all management, from the top down, before the changeover is made. This is a must, unless the desired objective is chaos compounded with confusion. It will undoubtedly take a significant amount of time to recondition the mental sets of an entire managerial staff, but this must be done before setting out on the new road, or the change is foredoomed to failure from the start.

The logical persons to whom to entrust this important task are competent behavioral scientists. It is better if they are permanent staff members, but if the company is too small to employ such personnel, some good consultants should be called in to do the job. And don't rush them. Give them a chance to familiarize themselves with the present setup *and* the people involved before they are forced to begin any re-educational program. They will then be able to judge the necessary scope and depth of their activities in swinging around the thinking of the management group. The changes are not minor; they should not be treated as such by anyone involved in the process. As in an MBO (management by objectives) installation, the preplanning may take more time than the actual setting up of the new procedures and changes in management activities. But it can be eminently worthwhile if done well.

Confusion of Relationships

It is small wonder that the manager who has spent a lifetime in the traditional forms of organizations finds himself lost when he is forced into a matrix for the first time. There is a nearly total reversal of his relationships with his own manager, his people, his peers, and other managers at higher levels in the organization.

For starters, the solid-line relationship becomes less important than dotted-line relationships. As things get rolling, he will spend more of his working time reporting to other managers in totally different parts of the organization than he spends reporting to his nominal boss. The underlying idea the manager must first absorb in conceptualizing the matrix is that his allegiance will be shifting with the various projects to which he is assigned. While he is working on one, he is in every sense responsible to the manager of *that* activity, and to *no other*, including even his own nominal boss. This is hard for many managers to accept, let alone adapt to well and smoothly.

Next, his peer relationships will undeniably become fuzzier than they formerly were. In moving around the organization from function to function, he will get to know more people slightly, but fewer intimately. He may find it harder to set up and maintain a good, in-depth reportage system as to what is going on in the enterprise at large. Not only will his close friendships with his peers gradually decline in number, but there will be an ebbing and flowing of sharp rivalries with peers as different projects vie for attention or priority rights to men, money, and materials. The manager newly introduced into a matrix may pass through a stage when he or she thinks of it more and more as a managerial jungle, where everything that moves is a potential enemy. This neurotic reaction should be recognized, met head-on, and subdued whenever it arises, or the manager will wind up with a permanently negative attitude, and his or her effectiveness will be lessened.

This matter of mental self-discipline is one of the most significant needs of the manager in a matrix. The first step toward resolution of the problem is to realize that all other managers in the organization are undergoing the same tensions and trauma. Yours is not a unique situation, but a common one indeed. After you have achieved this realization, talk it over with some of your peers, or even with your own manager. William Glasser's book *Reality Therapy** is based on the assumption that all our mental health problems arise from our failure to face reality in our everyday living. Once we have looked the enemy in the eye, we usually find that he is human, too, and in all likelihood no stronger than we are.

Another disturbing element mentioned earlier in this chapter is the frequent inversion of managerial roles encountered in the "fruit basket upset" of the matrix organization. For example, perhaps you were just "one of the boys" in a recently completed project; you were picked because you were sufficiently competent to make a contribution but were not assigned as the project manager. The next project that comes along lies in your particular specialty, and you receive the happy but rather disquieting news that you have been designated as project manager for it. As you look over the manning table, it is immediately apparent that one of the best-qualified

* New York: Harper & Row, 1965.

persons to pick for your team is the one to whom you were reporting a few days ago. You would be highly unusual if this didn't give you a few butterflies, but it is your clear duty to tab him as a member of the project team, and if this manager has assimilated the philosophy of the matrix organization, there will be no hesitancy in his acceptance of the assignment. After two or three times around, these role reversals become a part of the new way of life, and they will cease to upset you.

Another disturbing element that you will have to become accustomed to is the never-ending flow of new *non*managerial personnel you will have reporting to you from job to job. One of two things will happen: You will either become discouraged and give up any real attempt at getting to know your people, or you will suddenly intensify your efforts to become more intuitive and a quicker and smarter judge of people you have just met. It is earnestly to be hoped that you elect the latter alternative.

Early in the game, you will discover that much more coordinative effort is required of a manager in a matrix than has been necessary in the traditional organizations. Matrices are employed as organizational vehicles for complex types of operations. This means that less and less of the total job can be done by one group, while more and more cooperative efforts must be elicited to reach your goals. This is both good and bad. It is good because it will demand that you and all other managers become more and more cooperative on a continuing basis; it is bad because there are natural limits to how far a person can stretch himself in a dozen different directions at once. You will get so that you will feel like an amoeba, with a myriad of pseudopodia extending in all directions. Of course, your central concern—getting *your* job done success-fully—will remain unchanged during your orientation to the new scene.

All is not lost. Have hope. Be patient. After a certain period of time, which varies with the personal characteristics of the managers concerned, the new organizational concepts will begin to crystallize and fall into place. When this occurs, it will be immediately apparent that your panorama of the management arena is much broader than it had ever been before. The air will be clearer; your visibility will be miles greater; your concept of the job you have to do will be much clearer and more definite.

So far we have looked at only one side of a bright and shiny new coin—the disruption of your old ideas about the sanctity of the solid-line relationships between supervisor and employee. We still have to consider how *dotted*-line relation-ships differ in the matrix.

When Is a Dotted Line Not Dotted?

The most difficult readjustment a manager has to make when he enters a matrix organization is the reorientation of his think-ing about dotted-line relationships. Before, in the traditional organization, the dotted line represented simply a staff or liaison type of interaction. Now there is the possibility that a dotted line will suddenly disappear, and in its place there will jump up the hardest sort of solid line for the duration of a project. Moreover, the manager is told that he has dotted lines leading to every other function and discipline represented in the enterprise, and that these lines can undergo this transfor-mation at any time depending on the appearance of a need for his expertise.

Actually, the routine for accomplishing this transformation is quite simple. One department sees that it is going to need help from another department, or another group, in order to reach its objectives. They approach the manager of the discipline involved and explain their problem. According to the priorities that have been established for the jobs awaiting help, the new one is put into the hopper, and when its number comes up, the manager involved immediately assumes a position as a solid-line employee of the manager who needs help until the problem has been solved.

Yet there is a subtle difference between the relationship that evolves here and the old-fashioned "boss-subordinate" type of relationship. Although totally accountable and responsible to the manager of the project he is serving, the manager who has been called into service has something of the aura of a consultant, rather than that of a subordinate. It is recognized by everyone, although usually implicitly, that a person with a needed expertise has been called upon; the final relationship is not too different from that between a doctor and a patient.

Perhaps it would be useful here to give a concrete example of how this sort of project can develop. The manager of the materiel (purchasing) department of a large manufacturing organization was converting to MBO. He had six assistant managers reporting to him, and a total of some 250 members of management, spanning four echelons, within his operations. He turned to the Management Development Section of his division and asked its manager to assign an internal consultant on a part-time basis to help him get the matter off the ground. In his first interview with the person designated to respond to his need, the manager of the materiel department expressed his private fears that he was going to meet with concerted and serious resistance to his project from four of the managers who reported directly to him. His analysis was that these men feared (groundlessly) two things: that their control over their subdepartments would be weakened, and that they would be inundated in a flood of new paper work.

The consultant from MD estimated that he would be able to allocate one-third of his time to the project, since he had two other ongoing duties that he could neither evade nor delegate.

The manager and the consultant did some careful planning together. Their first objective was to indoctrinate the manager's assistants into the general theory and practice of MBO by a series of half-day conferences (to be accomplished within the next three months) that would culminate in each assistant manager's having come up with an acceptable set of objectives for his subgroup for the next six months. The estimate proved to be somewhat optimistic. It was closer to a year before all of the assistant managers had reported back to and negotiated with the manager a viable set of first-round objectives.

It had been decided that no effort would be made to carry the process down to the third echelon until the assistant managers had gone through their first set of objectives and had measured their success or lack of it. The boss and the consultant were both determined that they should have successful experiences in learning the method before carrying it down the line. This reasoning proved correct. Four of the assistants had remarkably good experiences and became converts to the methodology. The other two dragged their heels and were not so successful, thus remaining unsold on the concept. What finally brought them around was seeing how their peers were becoming jet-propelled and were getting some rather astonishing results with their subdepartments. The evidence persuaded them, and there developed much greater unity among the assistants than had ever existed before.

The next step was to have the assistants, with the aid and comfort of the MD consultant, prepare for a downward extension of the project and present guidelines to their subordinates. Here it became necessary to be much more aware of the coordination necessary among all subgroups, so that the major departmental objectives would not be obscured. Some problems in coordination did arise, but they did not prove to be insurmountable. One thing, however, was quite noticeable: The resistance at first evinced by the assistant managers was lacking in their subordinates, because they had observed what had happened to their bosses in the first couple of cycles of setting objectives and working to achieve them.

It was nearly three years before all four levels of management had been trained and the entire materiel department was truly operating under a viable MBO system. At the end of that time, however, the entire department had made such indisputable gains that it was singled out for special commendation and awards by the vice president and general manager of the division. Incidentally, on a personal basis, the MD consultant felt he was one of the big winners, since the project had given him an excellent chance to become thoroughly familiar with a new function, one about which he had been naive before. His disengagement from this long project occurred just in time for him to pick up a new assignment of liaison with Corporate Management Development in a personnel research effort they were launching.

These changing relationships in the matrix organization

provide some rare opportunities for managers to grow and develop in their professional life. Each new project will have its unique facets and will present new problems that invite innovative solutions and fresh approaches. It's an exciting way to spend your business life.

Priorities and Interpersonal Relationships

There is one aspect of the matrix organization that is worthy of special attention because of its trickiness. More often than we would like, there are collision courses between the priorities of the projects' needs as they arise. For example, a large airframe manufacturer had adopted the project (matrix) type of organization for the production of several models of commercial jets. They had set up a relatively small but extremely sharp group of engineering research personnel (numbering some fifty engineers) as a separate organization, with a manager and five section chiefs. Several of the models had some problems in aerodynamics at the same time. They all landed on the doorstep of the engineering research manager nearly simultaneously, and each of the project managers was adamant that his problem should be the first to be attacked by engineering research. This led to some serious confrontations among the various project managers, all of whom were at the same level of management.

Technically speaking, the manager of engineering research was at the same level in the hierarchy as the project managers, but practically speaking this just wasn't so. Although his function was extremely important, it didn't lead directly to the production of any of the different jet models, and he had considerably less clout than the project managers. He became the man in the middle in no uncertain terms.

Whatever decision he made was sure to be met with storms of protest. For example, one of the jet models was the indisputable leader in its field in the industry, and at the time was really the only model making large profits for the enterprise. Should its needs be subordinated to the needs of another model that was being launched two years too late, after a competitor had become well-entrenched in its area of the market? It was doubtful that this model would *ever* reach the breakeven point, since the total market was approaching saturation. But the model was already running late, and the company had invested heavily in its development.

It was not possible simply to enlarge the engineering research group magically by bringing in new bodies. The people presently in the group were experts in the various areas of research, through a combination of natural bent and aptitude; they had an intense interest in the types of problem solving they were called on to do; they had years of experience in a variety of similar situations, and had therefore a mass of historical data to consult when making decisions on research problems. You don't just reach out at random and find people like this whenever your group happens to need them.

In this kind of Mexican standoff, the procedure is, of course, to buck the decisions to higher levels of management, who then assume responsibility for assigning priorities and setting up timetables. Once again, whatever decision is finally reached is likely to prove abrasive to the relationships between some of the project managers, but at least the onus for the decisions is on "them"—the impersonal and hazy members of mahogany row.

Successful project managers become an elite crew, small in number but of immense power as they pile up an impressive array of achievements. Their repeated competition with their peers is quite likely to engender aversions that become ingrained and habitual, so that in effect their polarizations are permanent. This is not the most desirable of happenings, but it is fairly predictable psychologically.

On the other hand, these project managers have a tendency to pick up cadres of subordinates who, after continued and repeated testing, have passed the hurdles and are considered permanent members of the particular team. This means that as a project manager finishes one assignment and goes on to the next, he will most certainly take many of his subordinates with him to the new venture, and semipermanent working teams evolve through this process.

Within these semipermanent groups, relationships tend to be tightly cohesive, and cooperation runs high. The project managers will be intensely dedicated to the mastery of each problem as it appears, and the team spirit produced works wonders as far as accomplishment goes. In these groups there is also (as previously mentioned) a polyglot mixture of comings and goings of team members with special credentials in areas in which outside help is needed.

It should be noted that the assignment of priorities to different projects running concurrently gives birth to a caste system that is not entirely admirable or desirable for overall organizational health. When the ranking of the various projects becomes clear, the status of the team members will vary widely from group to group. The members of the team picked to handle the most glamorous and highest-priority project acquire a special aura that other groups never achieve. This is not the best possible situation, but it is unavoidable in the matrix organization, and will continue for the foreseeable future.

On balance, however, we have the fact that the *overall* status and rankings of all members of a matrix organization are higher than in the more traditional and less glamorous kinds of structures. Inherent in the matrix approach to management is a sense of challenge and excitement which permeates the thinking and actions of all the members of the enterprise and which is conducive to their putting forth their best efforts. Good team members have a way of rising above their personal feelings about peers in order to get the job done satisfactorily. When a manager can truly subordinate his personal feelings about others to the success of the project, he has reached true maturity as a manager and can be trusted to make decisions that will be functional and in the best interests of all concerned. We shall examine next this matter of the general tonus of the matrix organization, and the philosophy the manager needs in order to be successful in its operation.

The Best for the Most

If there is any single concept that would express the meaning of the matrix organization, it is the traditional idea of "the best for the most." Call it cooperation, teamwork, concentration of group effort toward the achievement of group goals, or what will you, this is the theme of the setting up of such an organizational structure.

Ideologically, this assumes a kind of restructuring of every individual's personal sense of values on a higher and more altruistic plane. We cannot afford to allow personal ambition to guide our activities within the work structure, since in the long run this would be subversive to our best interests because of the probable failure of the group to reach its final objectives completely and in the most economical manner.

Every action a manager undertakes must first be subjected to a scrutiny to assure him/her that it would be most productive for the matrix, as well as for himself. If it cannot pass this test, the action should be abandoned.

Item: It is natural to want to receive full credit for those things we do—personal credit, that is. Many times in the matrix organization this is not possible, since the final achievements will generally be spread over so many people that the individual achievements cannot be effectively winnowed out and reported.

Item: The manager's planning must be done from a different basis, and with a different set of objectives. No longer can he center all his energies and thinking on what his or her little group will be doing; intergroup coordination and cooperation become the central keys to getting where we want to go. In other words, we must give as much consideration to what is good for our peer groups as we do to what is advantageous for our own subgroup.

Item: The manager's approach to the training of his people will be different than in the traditional kinds of organizational structures. He must inculcate into their thinking, early and quite indelibly, the same ideas he has absorbed about the subgroup subordinating its selfish objectives to the overall goals of the entire enterprise.

Item: If these things are effectively accomplished, there will be significant changes in both the thinking and the attitudes of middle and upper management. Stratification will be blurred to an extent undreamed of in former times. I have already mentioned that in passing from project to project there will be many inversions of leadership, because of the differing degrees of expertise held by managers in different fields and disciplines. This will bring many changes in the way managers regard others who are nominally "above" or "below" them in the hierarchy.

Item: No matrix organization can be successful if there is any significant or continuing blockage of free and open two-way communications in all directions and at all levels. The timing is too delicate, and the results too dependent on this open communication, for any breakdown in communications to be tolerable. This becomes perhaps the chief onus of every manager in the matrix; *nothing*, either of omission or commission, can be tolerated that will choke off a smooth flow of the necessary data in all directions.

Item: Managerial objectivity gains new importance in the firm's operations. No personalities can ever be allowed to become dominant in making the necessary decisions for action. This does not mean that the managerial force will or should ever become a group of emotional zombies; it does, however, imply that emotionalism and personal concerns must be completely subsumed to the welfare of the organization as an entity. This is unquestionably the most difficult single adjustment you as a manager will be forced to make in learning to live in a matrix. Once this has been accomplished, however, the sailing will be much smoother from there on out.

THE MANAGER: NERVE CENTER OF INTERPERSONAL RELATIONSHIPS

THE CENTRAL THESIS of this short book has been that interpersonal relationships are of crucial importance to the success of any business venture. We have looked at various permutations and combinations of one-to-one and group relationships that can have an effect, either good or bad, on the communications and operations of the enterprise. One fact emerges from this examination with irrefutable clarity: The manager is the nerve center who receives, controls, and directs the currents that affect his success and the success of the enterprise. It is the manager's sensitivity to the nerve impulses he receives, and his judiciousness in choosing the impulses he transmits, that will determine such things as the most effective manning tables for the project at hand, the most effective and viable team relationships, the reduction of abrasive confrontations between inimical personalities, the synergistic effects of welding good teams, and the overview from the manager's seat that will enable him to achieve "the best for the most."

One thing every modern manager must remember is the following intuitive (but only recently formulated) law of adult learning: No amount of knowledge will effect any significant change in an organization of adults unless it is accompanied by action. We can only truly "know" something when we have practiced it until, so to speak, the synaptic resistance to the passage of the nerve messages has been reduced below the conscious level. We must habituate ourselves to being the traffic directors of interpersonal relationships within our groups to the point where our activity in this area is automatic. As long as we still have to stop and think about it, we are not totally effective in this critical aspect of our job.

However, we can derive comfort from the fact that the application of a small amount of basic theory to a large amount of repetitive practice will result in effects we could never have dreamed possible before. Success is not only habit forming but addictive—and every good manager hungers for success in the field to which he has dedicated himself.